LOST AT SEA

10 UNBELIEVABLE SHIPWRECK STORIES ON THE HIGH SEAS AND HOW THEY SURVIVED AGAINST ALL ODDS

MODERN DAILY

LOST AT SEA

10 UNBELIEVABLE SHIPWRECK STORIES ON THE HIGH SEAS AND HOW THEY SURVIVED AGAINST ALL ODDS

MODERN DAILY

Exclusive Bonus Content

Dear Reader,

Thank you for your purchase. As an appreciation for your purchase, we added a **free audiobook download** for you. These files are available exclusively for free as .mp3 and can be downloaded by scanning the code below.

Listen for free on any smartphone, tablet, or PC device!

We thank you, valued reader, for choosing this book. We hope that it exceeds expectation as the author and team worked with utmost care to bring a quality project to life.

Should you encounter any issues, please don't hesitate to reach out — we are here to ensure you are fully satisfied with your purchase and look forward to meeting you inside the pages.

Love,

*Free bonus audiobook product may differ from images shown.

Lost At Sea

10 Unbelievable Shipwreck Stories on the High Seas and How They Survived Against All Odds

Copyright © 2025
by Modern Daily

moderndaily. PRESS

All rights reserved. **No part of this publication** may be reproduced, stored or transmitted **in any form or by any means**, electronic, mechanical, photocopying, recording, scanning, or otherwise without written permission from the publisher. It is illegal to copy this book, post it to a website, or distribute it by any other means without permission.

Disclaimers and Terms of Use: The publisher and author do not warrant or represent that the contents within are accurate and disclaim all warranties and is not liable for any damages whatsoever. Although all attempts were made to verify information, they do not assume any responsibility for errors, omissions, or contrary interpretation of the subject matter contained within as perceived slights of peoples, persons, organizations are unintentional and information contained within should not be used as a source of legal, business, accounting, financial, or other professional advice. Publisher and author has no responsibility for the persistence or accuracy of URLs for external or third-party Internet Websites referred to in this publication and does not guarantee that any content on such Websites is, or will remain, accurate or appropriate.

Product names, logos, brands, and other trademarks featured or referred to within this publication are the property of their respective trademark holders and are not sponsored, approved, licensed, or endorsed by any of their licensees or affiliates.

CONTENT

Introduction ～～ 9

Alexander Selkirk ～～ 11

The Mignonette:
   Story of Survival of the Fittest ～～ 19

Mary Celeste. Where Are You? ～～ 27

The Man Who Hoped for the Better ～～ 35

A Couple Lost is a Couple Found ～～ 43

USS Indianapolis: The Final Voyage ～～ 51

Outrunning Death:
   The Louis Zamperini Story ～～ 59

The Essex: A Whaling Tragedy ～～ 69

Meet The Robertsons: The Family at Sea ～～ 79

The Expedition of All Expeditions:
Thor Heyerdahl and the Kon-Tiki ～～ 89

Conclusion ～～ 99

Works Cited ～～ 101

About Us ～～ 107

INTRODUCTION

Stories are meant to be the change, creating a ripple effect. They are supposed to be enabling something or instigating something. They are intended to move people, motivate them out of being stagnant, and propel them into active participants in life. When researching what to put in this article, I wanted to choose stories that can impact people in as significant ways as possible. I say significant because some stories have an impact, but that doesn't mean the effect is as needed or remembered as we want it to be. You'll forget it someday soon, but I don't want that. I would like these stories to stay with you for a long time, and I think these stories are just that - something to impact you, the readers, meaningfully.

One of the stories I picked is Alexander Selkirk's story. The other is the tragedy that befell the Mignonette, specifically Richard Parker. These two stories are famous for many reasons, and most of them are different reasons from each other. However, they do share the same tone of survival. These stories, after all, are about one's survival at sea.

The sea is not an easy terrain that you can simply traverse to find another path back home. No. The sea is much more cruel than that. Swimming takes up energy, so you can't swim for days at a time. Where on land, you can rest. You won't be able to rest in the sea because you won't have a place to. The ocean is just water, and the only land where you can rest when lost is on the ocean floor. Which, for self-explanatory reasons, is not an option.

These two stories are different. One account is inspirational; it talks about how even when you're lost, you can still find the strength to want to survive without meaning to find it.

In Alexander Selkirk's case, he found God, and his faith was enough for him to fight to survive. I'm not saying religion is a saving grace, and I know that religion is not necessarily needed for some people, including myself.

However, the story is a commentary that even if you don't look for the will to live or a purpose to live, it will still find you. In this sense, the story is positively inspirational.

The second story is very different from the first, the story of the Mignonette. It's not inspirational. However, it does teach anyone who reads it a lesson. It teaches that every action has a consequence and that you will not know how strong you are lest you are faced with an impossible decision.

Cannibalism is no joke, and it is obvious the men on that yacht thought so, as it took them some days to make a choice. Still, remember that everything has consequences, and you can't say how well your resolve is unless it has been tested.

So now, you will read these two stories and others. I hope you find them as meaningful as I found them.

ALEXANDER SELKIRK:
THE REAL LIFE OF ROBINSON CRUSOE

"There is nothing more enticing, disenchanting, and enslaving than the life at sea."

– Joseph Conrad

So many people were thought of to be the inspiration for the stories of Robinson Crusoe. It has been speculated but never resolved for years until people named one man the instigator. His name was Alexander Selkirk, sometimes referred to as Alexander Selcraig (since he changed his name during his time at sea). Alexander was the seventh son of John Selcraig and Euphan Mackie. He was born in Largo, located in Fife, Scotland. He was born specifically in Drumochie, near the west end of Largo, in 1676.

While still in school, he was an intelligent student who excelled in his navigation lessons. However, as bright as he was, he was still involved in some usual childish mischief, which was only enabled by his mother, who kept these things from his father. John, unlike Euphan, was strict beyond belief. While he was the disciplinarian, Euphan was the optimist, hoping that her husband would be less of a hothead regarding lessons once Alexander came into their lives.

Euphan, being an optimist, encouraged Alexander's dreams to go off to sea. It caused a lot of fights in the household since John just wanted Alexander to stay and help with the family trade business. The arguments became so intense that John threatened to disown Alexander. By eighteen, however, he left his home to go to sea and stayed there for six years.

However, there were no documents to prove this statement, only the words of people who passed down this story.

He was said to be with the Buccaneers in the South Seas during that time.

By the time it was 1701, he was back in Largo again and maybe had an even "worse" attitude in his father's and brothers' eyes. It came to the point where the church elders had to step in and intervene. So, Alexander left as soon as the weather permitted him to. He first left for England to return to the South Seas.

He boarded the ship of Captain Dampier, whose mission was to go through the river La Plata to get to Buenos Ayres to obtain money. Due to this mission, two ships were equipped: St. George and Cinque Ports Galley. The latter was where Alexander Selkirk became the sailing master. They arrived at Kinsale, Ireland, on May 18, 1703 (while St. George docked on April 30, 1703).

When they all arrived at the island of Madeira to retrieve gold on May 25, 2023, they did not set the anchor down and made their way. Instead, they sent a small boat to the shore to gather information. When the ship returned, they discovered the money was safe at Teneriffe.

It took months – nearing a full year - for them to find money and other supplies. However, they did not get this through the usual legal means, and they became pirates through their adventures because the crown legalized them.

The Day he Decided to Stay

Alexander Selkirk was the sailing master, basically the navigator, for the Cinque Ports Gallery (the ship's name). Even though he had an adventurous heart, his view on many things changed when he arrived on a deserted island off the coast of Valparaiso, Chile, in October 1704. After many months with Captain Dampier (leader of the expedition) and his numerous adventures aboard the Cinque Ports Gallery, he finally snapped.

Before everything went down, he was sailing away around the seas with this band of people who were legal pirates, as made by the British Crown at that time. He was on good terms with his captain; however, his relationship with the Lieutenant, Thomas Stradling, was compromised because of the attacks that started. It was compromised before the attacks happened, as the original Captain of the Cinque Ports died, Stradling was promoted, but so was Selkirk. Their positions caused them to clash. The fact that Strendling wouldn't make the desperately needed repairs caused some distress within Alexander Selkirk.

Due to the number of times he and his crewmates encountered different Spanish vessels, the ship docked at the uninhabited islands of Juan Fernandez, about 400 miles from the coast of Chile, so they may have time and resources to restock on provisions. However, Selkirk had some reservations about going out to sea soon because of the number of things they needed to repair their battle-damaged ship.

They did not even "park" the vessels; they sent out a smaller boat to grab the provisions, and because of this, he demanded to be left on the island. The ship's Lieutenant, Thomas Stradling, an arrogant man (according to Alexander Selkirk), approved his demands and left him on the island. Selkirk grabbed his belongings and other things like a musket, bullets, gunpowder, carpenter tools, extra clothing and bedding, tobacco, a hatchet, and a Bible. He thought other men and crewmates would join him in this stand, but they didn't. Alexander regretted his decision and asked if he could board the ship again. Lieutenant Stradling disapproved of his begging, leaving him to rot on the island.

At first, he was happy to be alone on the island, but it was only a fleeting moment. As he watched and heard the ship he'd lived in for a year sail away, his dread fell in, and he could not believe that he was alone on the island, with no company at all. An article from J. Howell's book, "The Life and Adventures of Alexander Selkirk," explained Selkirk as he watched his ship sail away, abandoning him on an island with nothing but the few things he brought but leaving him without a will to live.

Alone and Unafraid: How Alexander Remained Sane

What happened to Alexander Selkirk was actually shared among sailors. The term for it is "being marooned." Typically, isolated people are left with nothing – no equipment or provisions. It was a death sentence to unruly sailors. However, Alexander Selkirk broke the usual pattern for it.

He asked to be marooned (although he regretted it) and then was able to bring with him enough equipment and provisions to survive for some time. So, it was not a death sentence for him, although perhaps people thought it was a crueler faith because he had the means to survive longer than the usual time frame for someone in his position.

At first, Selkirk was devastated. He barely ate or slept; his mind was too full of despair at being alone on a deserted island. Soon enough, however, he did find his way back to becoming a functioning human being again. Well, as much as the situation can make you into a functional human being. "No man is an island" is a cliché that must be why Selkirk was so distraught at first. He is a fighter, and he did fight indeed.

It was the beginning of October in the year 1704, and seeing as he was in a tropical climate, Selkirk's usual sailing outfit was destroyed in the weather. So, he fashioned clothes from goat skins, one of the many things he was fortunate to bring to his desolate island.

Since he was alone on the island, he was alone with his thoughts. Some thoughts were not helpful, others were. One of the better thoughts was his religious education from childhood; since he had a bible, he reconnected and found comfort and hope. He started to fight again.

Once he had hope again, he built two huts from the wood of the pimento trees around the island. He made furniture as well, including a bed. However, he could not build it all, so he improvised. His bedroom became a chapel for him.

Alexander Selkirk continued and created a routine for himself each day. He would start the day by singing a psalm, reading a passage from the bible, and then ending with a prayer. Then, throughout the day, he worked on nothing and everything to ensure he survived. Once the day was over, he would sleep to rest for the next day of survival. His devotion to his faith kept him going and pushed him to survive.

Selkirk built two huts for himself. One was his home, and the other was a smaller one that became his kitchen. Since much of the island was deserted, animals still lived there. Tamed goats surrounded his home.

He used the Indian method of starting a fire: rubbing two pieces of wood (from the pimento trees) together until it sparked a flame. He could find food and scavenged all around the island for it. For example, since he had no access to bread, he used a cabbage palm instead. He used the plant life on the island to sustain him physically.

Because of this newfound peace of mind, he enjoyed life alone on this deserted island. He found another way of life that helped him through this tough time in his life through God and his belief in him—according to a report by Rogers, who was one of the people who saved him, he was a better man because of the faith he found on that island. Perhaps being scared and alone was just the push he needed to be close to his God and his faith. Either way, it saved him.

Of course, not everything was rainbows and sunshine. He did encounter some difficulties along the way. He found some animal problems, and the island could only sustain someone for so long despite him being just one man. Still, he was able to overcome them with his positive attitude.

He learned several skills that helped him survive, which came in handy when he was finally found by another ship. It was one of the reasons why his rescuers gladly brought him in; he helped them stay alive by what he saw and learned on the isolated island.

He survived for a long time on the island. He lasted until 1709, when he was finally found and brought back to the world of the living.

Sailor Till the End

However content as Alexander Selkirk may have been on his little island, he was still on the lookout for passing ships. He is still human and needs a way to return to civilization. In January of 1709, there was one ship that was spotted. The boat of William Rogers, a British captain, found him.

The ship's name was "The Duke". Finally, Selkirk was filled with a new kind of hope, the hope of being welcomed back into the world and home – his actual, true home.

When he caught sight of the ship, he hurried to prepare a makeshift raft with a fire blazing and a white flag on it to show them that someone was on the deserted island. Once the boat pulled itself onto the beach, Selkirk was ecstatic. When he boarded the ship, Dampier, his former captain, who led the expedition that started this whole debacle in the first place, the leader of the Cinque Ports Gallery, was onboard and gave him a beautiful character recommendation.

Due to that endorsement, he was immediately placed into the sailor's crew. However, more than just the recommendation helped him stay aboard that ship.

Still, they did not sail off right away. They stayed for a while, resting and stocking up. Selkirk made good with the recommendation given to him by Dampier, and he showed his skills in hunting and medicine – basically, all the survival knowledge he gained throughout the years he stayed on the island.

This just proved to William Rogers and his crew that the recommendation that he was given was genuine. Once they were ready, Alexander Selkirk packed his prized belongings, which included the bible, and left the island.

Alexander Selkirk was not only found and brought back to the land of the living, but he was also saved in more ways than one and by more people than just William Rogers and his crew. In his eyes, he was also saved by his God. He came back to the world as a new man who later inspired the stories of Robinson Crusoe.

THE MIGNONETTE:
STORY OF SURVIVAL OF THE FITTEST

"Who wants to die? Everything struggles to live. Look at that tree growing up there out of that grating. It gets no sun, and water only when it rains. It's growing out of sour earth. And it's strong because its hard struggle to live makes it strong. My children will be strong that way."

- Betty Smith.

Cannibalism is a concept that has been infamous in human society for years. It has existed throughout the years, and the people who partake in actions of cannibalism have struck terror and fear in the people of the community. Cannibalism, also called anthropophagy, is the practice of eating your kind's flesh. This is typically seen in animals. However, what makes it actual cannibalism is when it is humans partaking in another human's flesh. However, in history, cannibalism is normal. Many years ago, it could be found in South American tribal customs. It can also be found in recent stories for the mere purpose of survival.

The story of the Mignonette, a yacht that carried four people on its body to sail in 1884. The boat was a decent size, around 52 feet long, and was designed for coastal sailings and not for long voyages. However, the man who bought the Mignonette lived in Sydney, Australia, while the yacht was in England.

The person who bought the yacht was John Want, a Sydney Barrister and Commodore of the Sydney Yacht Club. Although he did not sail the craft himself, he hired four people to sail it for him so they could bring it to him.

He hired Captain Thomas Dudley, and the Captain hired three more people for this venture. These three people are Edwin Stephens, Edmund Brooks, and Richard Parker. Richard was seventeen, the youngest and most inexperienced aboard the yacht. Sadly, he would be the victim of this story.

Survival of the fittest is a concept that has been introduced previously to everyone. It has been there since Charles Darwin mentioned the term in his book. However, to experience it at its most primitive state is something to be scared of.

When the Mignonette left port in 1884, their survival of the fittest occurred. Cannibalism, sadly, was their way of surviving. What's more, as much as most people would think they would never do what they did, it is different when you are in the situation. "You won't know until you try it" could be a saying that fits the scenario. You won't know what you will do unless you try to experience that same experience.

The Mignonette set sail on May 19, 1884. That day, the four sailors had no idea what they would face; they thought they knew, but evidently, they did not prepare enough for the catastrophe. Cannibalism is no joke; it was necessary for the men's survival. It is a sad truth of this survival story that everyone has to face at one point.

A Delivery Gone Wrong

The four men's mission was simple: deliver the Mignonette to John Want, who lived in Australia. Most of them were experienced sailors, and even though Richard Parker was not experienced, his family was not estranged to the ways of being at sea. So, he knew the theory; he just needed to apply what he knew. Which he did; they all did their best to survive. However, the best of the three older men paved the way to the tragic end of the youngest.

The Mignonette was not built for long travels, but they had to try anyway. One night, a large wave came about and destroyed the vessel's Lee Bulwark, the yacht's defensive wall. The Mignonette was quickly filling up with water, and they had to act quickly, or else they would drown right then and there.

The captain, Thomas Dudley, already figured that the ship was at its end, so he ordered his tiny crew onto the lifeboat, which was just 13 feet in size. The yacht sank to the bottom of the sea not long after they got off it. However, not all hope was lost at first. They could salvage enough navigational equipment and some tins of turnips to last them for some time.

Survival was hard; they had to fend off sharks with their oars to ensure they weren't eaten. The crew was so far away from any land, around 700 miles from civilization. They had about two tins of turnips, and the first one lasted until July 7. They had to scavenge their food, which included a turtle they found on the sea.

They thought their luck was improving, seeing as they found a food source other than turnips, but it was not enough to last them long. They resorted to drinking seawater when they had no rainwater to quench their thirst. Even with the risks of drinking seawater (the risk of being fatal), they thought it better than dying of thirst or hallucinating from dehydration. Plain and simple, they were desperate to survive. They were so desperate that they were willing to take any risks.

The last can of turnips was done by July 15. They became so desperate from thirst that they drank their urine. By July 17, the youngest, Richard Parker, got sick from their experiment on drinking seawater. That day marked their 19th day at sea. Still, despite everything that has happened so far, it is not the worst thing that has happened just yet. Their desperation to live became the reason behind this story's tragedy. The need to survive was far greater than any of their morals, which is how humanity is when faced with the end of their lives.

A Delivery For Survival

It is customary for sailors to draw lots when deciding when it comes to sacrificing someone from the crew. It was discussed during the days when Richard Parker was sick and nearing death. The discussion continued for some days, as this kind of discussion should be. Initially, the captain wanted to draw lots to see who to sacrifice.

However, they started to talk to each other. Every single one of them had their own families (wives and children) to get home to. Except for Richard. They all had a chance of survival. Except, again, for Richard. The debate started July 17, the day they ran out of food, and the day Richard fell ill.

Edmund Brooks was against the whole sacrificial lamb cannibalism thing to begin with. He didn't want to partake in any of it, so he stayed out of the discussion. However, he did not stop the discussion. He was a witness to the reasoning of Captain Dudley and Edwin Stephens.

They talked about how they needed to get back home to their families, how their families depended on them to provide, and if they died, who would help their families survive? Then, they discussed how Richard was already sick and dying more than any of them.

Then, they decided it was better to kill Richard before he died and use his blood to help them survive. It would be better for everyone. At least, that is what they told themselves.

So, after days of discussion and pondering on whether they should do it or not, one day, they finally decided they had to do it.

Dudley and Stephens slashed Richard's throat, even though he begged them for mercy. Still standing on his not wanting to be a part of this decision, Brooks looked away as they killed the 17-year-old boy.

They poured the young man's blood into a tin where they used to keep the turnips and drank his blood for their thirst. Unable to hold himself off any longer, Brooks crumbled and drank the blood. Still, they didn't even stop there.

The next thing they did was butcher the poor kid and ate his body as a supplement for meat. The heart and the liver were the first things they ate. Then, they divided the flesh and rationed it for as long as possible. Everything else that couldn't be used was thrown overboard. There was nothing left of Richard's body after this story.

Of course, things didn't get much better because they were still out at sea with no place to store the boy's meat. So it began to rot. But their luck changed when they spotted a ship at a distance on the 24th day of being stranded. On July 29, they saw a German boat called Montezuma and were saved. Or so they thought. The people on the Montezuma brought them to Falmouth, Cornwall, on September 6.

Once they arrived, they gave their report on what happened to them, as stated under the Merchant Shipping Act; because of their being at sea, they thought their act of cannibalism was going to be pardoned.

However, they were asked how they killed the boy. They told the Sergeant it was with a pen, which he took into evidence. The three men were planning to reunite with their families when they were detained.

Dudley, Brooks, and Stephens were brought to court on September 8 to try and defend themselves from their cannibalism. Their captain was sure that the magistrates would see reason and pardon them. The hearing started and was led by Sir William Harcourt, who saw their act not only as cannibalism but also as taking advantage of a minor and murdering him.

The story got so big that it attracted a crowd, and in that crowd was Richard's brother. What surprised everyone was that the brother sided with the three men who killed his blood. He defended them, saying that they did what they had to do. He could see their side more than a court could because he was also a seafarer.

While the court was deciding, they were bailed out and met their families until they had to go back and face the court's decision about what would happen to them. Will their crime be pardoned, or will they suffer the consequences of their survival decision?

The Final Call

The three men were on trial for the Murder of Richard Parker. The trial went on for a long time. The jury found themselves unable to convict Brooks of the same crime as Dudley and Stephens since he did not kill the boy. He did not hold Richard down as Stephens did. He did not slit the kid's throat with a pen like Dudley did.

So he was pardoned, and the other two were found guilty of murder. Nevertheless, their findings were more complicated than what it seemed. Since the jury was reluctant to pass the final judgment, they did not call it. Rather, the jury was replaced by five judges who convicted the two of murder instead. However, they all knew it would not push through, seeing as the crowd sympathized with them - including the victim's brother.

Still, Dudley and Stephens waited for days for what would happen to them. By law, they were not pardoned, but by the jury and the majority, they were. They were seen not exactly as murderers and most definitely not as victims. People simply understood their situation, so it was hard to decide when they didn't know how to feel about what happened to them.

So, at the end of it all, Home Security decided to just give them six months of imprisonment for their actions. They were sent to the Halloway Prison prison, where they served their time. After that, they could return home to their families and live out the rest of their lives.

No accounts were found after this, and whether they were at peace with their decision is unknown. It is not known whether they were living their lives happily or not. What is known of this story is the horrors of what is faced at sea: the choices that need to be made, the tests of your morals, and the showing of how strong one's resolve is when shoved into an impossible and horrible situation.

MARY CELESTE, WHERE ARE YOU?

"I'll never know and neither will you of the life you don't choose. We'll only know whatever that sister life was, it was important an beautiful and not ours. It was the ghost ship that didn't carry us. There's nothing to do but salute it to the thrift shop."

– Cheryl Strayed.

Have you ever heard of ghost ships? These ships are tied to supernatural stories from sailors' words. These ships are usually abandoned because of the stories. Or they are sometimes still being used despite the warnings of most sailors. These ghost ships range in stories over time. Ghost ships are usually ships that have been wrecked by the supernatural because of something inexplicably tragic happening aboard them. There are several stories wherein ghost ships are the star: the stories of the Flying Dutchman Ship and the Queen Mary cruise ship, for example. However, the focus of this article will be the story of the Mary Celeste.

The Mary Celeste's disappearance story is one of the prime examples of a ghost ship. The Mary Celeste was an American ship built during the 1860s in the Nova Scotian Hamlet of Spencer's Island. It was also known as "Brigantine," for it was a dual mast vessel, and the ship was first known as "Amazon."

The haunting story of the Mary Celeste started when they embarked on a voyage on November 7, 1872. At the start, they had seven crew members, including Captain Benjamin Spooner Briggs, his wife, Sarah, and their daughter, Sophia, who was two years old. The ship weighed 292 tons when it left port, and after two weeks, it arrived in Azores, its last known location before it disappeared. It was found by the people aboard the Del Gratia ship later on, on December 5, 1872, floating across the Atlantic Ocean near the Azores Islands in Portugal.

The captain of the Dei Gratia ship, Captain David Morehouse, was a close friend of Captain Briggs. He could recognize the Mary Celeste right away, and his crew thought there were people onboard, so they did their best to help the ship stabilize and bring the people on it home. To their surprise, it was empty when they got on the boat. Yet, there were no signs of struggle or violence. Their possessions were intact but it was just abandoned. As if everyone on the boat just disappeared into thin air.

Captain Morehouse searched the vicinity for any signs of life, but there was none. When the Dei Gratia returned to report what they found, the British court debated whether to give them the money discovered in the Mary Celeste.

However, one person, Attorney General Frederick Solly-Flood, suspected some foul play, so the money was withheld. After a few months, no evidence was found of his suspicion, so they gave the members of the Dei Gratia 46,000 dollars.

To this day, no one knows what happened to the Mary Celeste. It has been a mystery, and it will stay that way for some time.

History Before the Legend

The Mary Celeste was not always the "Mary Celeste." When it was first built, it was named the "Amazon," The Amazon had many troubles it had to overcome. It did not have a smooth sailing past, as much as it did not have a smooth sailing present. Over the years since it was built, it had some unsuccessful voyages. In June 1861, the Amazon was captained by Captain McLellan. The Amazon sailed to the Five Islands of Nova Scotia, where it was meant to ship a load of timber to London. Suddenly, though, while they were traveling to London, Captain McLellan got sick, and it kept getting worse until he died. He was the first of three captains to have died onboard the Amazon.

The next captain was Captain John Nutting Parker. He took the lead on the voyage when the Amazon collided with a set of fishing equipment and another ship while they were sailing across the English Channel. However, the Amazon survived while the other ship did not. Captain Parker continued being the captain after a few years, wherein the Amazon became a strict trading vessel.

After Captain Parker, the new captain was William Thomspon. He was in charge of the Amazon until 1867, wherein his reign was quiet until a storm hit their travels off the coast of Cape Breton Island early in October.

The ship was abandoned and then found by Alexander McBean, a Glace Bay, Nova Scotia resident. McBean found this opportunity and sold it to a local businessman who traded it to Richard W. Haines, a mariner based in New York. He spent some money on the repairs of the Amazon and then rechristened it as the Mary Celeste.

In October of 1969, the ship was sold to a man named James H. Winchester. According to the records, the ship remained stagnant, as it did not sail for trade or other purposes until 1872.

At that time, the ship received a new captain. His name was Captain Benjamin Spooner Briggs, who became known as the Captain of the Mary Celeste, the ship that disappeared.

The reason for the Mary Celeste's voyage was that it was meant to transport 1,700 alcohol casks to the Italian province of Genoa before 1872 ended. As stated earlier, the Mary Celeste left port on November 7, 1872. It was supposed to land on Genoese soil,

Speculations and Theories

Strait by the Dei Gratia ship. The Dei Gratia ship left New York a week after the Mary Celeste left its port.

It has been years since the disappearance of the Mary Celeste ship, and until now, people are not entirely sure of what happened. There are many theories and speculations about the possible reasons why the ship disappeared, why the people on board the vessel are nowhere to be found, and why the boat was drifting along the waters with no one steering it.

However, there are no guesses that stick the landing enough for people to call it the truth of what happened. The theories have ranged from realistic to mystical, from sea monsters to sea myths. Some views are as logical as they can be, for example, a pirate raid, but they still do not support the other findings on that ship, such as if it were a pirate raid, why are the belongings of the missing people still intact?

Alcohol. Some theories revolve around the reality that the alcohol casks were the problem and the reason for the abandonment of the ship. People believe that Captain Briggs thought the casks would explode and commanded everyone to abandon the ship because of it.

When the ship was found, nine barrels of alcohol were uncovered by the cloth, and there was a rope near it that dangled near the water that helped this theory, but it did not solidify it. People thought that because of the climate of the Azores, the heat would be enough to create an explosion with the alcohol. However, this was debunked even more when the reports stated no fume smells in the air.

Furthermore, the report stated that nine casks were empty. These nine were made of red oak and not white oak. The difference is that red oak's wood is more porous, which means it has more possibility of having leak spots.

Another possible theory is that the two German brothers aboard the ship, Volkert and Boye Lorenzen, are thought to be the reason for the ship's state, seeing as none of their belongings were found on the Mary Celeste the day the ship was floating adrift. However, the brothers' relatives told the people that the Lorenzen brothers lost their belongings in a shipwreck in 1872, and they did not have any motive to harm the other crew members.

Attorney General Solly-Flood had another theory as well. Solly-Flood thought that maybe the weather was to blame for all this chaos and tragedy. According to the records in his hand, Captain Briggs changed the course of the Mary Celeste to go northward of Santa Maria Island the day before the ship arrived at the Azores.

The ship's last entry was that of them facing rough waters and disastrous winds. Although this theory is very plausible, another one counteracted this, saying that because of the last shipment, which was coal, and since coal dust and construction debris came along, it might have contaminated the ship's pumps, causing it to malfunction. Captain Briggs must have told everyone to abandon the ship because the ship might sink, well, according to this theory.

If all these theories are very realistic, the mystical ones heavily revolve around the Bermuda Triangle. The Bermuda Triangle is an area in the Atlantic Ocean where people have been known to disappear when they pass through it. Some people believe that the Mary Celeste accidentally came across that area, so they mysteriously disappeared.

Another mystical theory can be found in the story written by Sir Arthur Conan Doyle. He stated in the book that "the ghost ship fell victim to an ex-slave seeking vengeance." (S.P., 2023). Other theories also involve aliens and ghosts. Still, there are no accounts of the people who believed this and why they did. Perhaps it is because there is still no hard proof to strengthen their claims besides the legends of what they think took the ship, such as the Bermuda Triangle.

Due to the mystery, there was eventually an investigation chronicled called "The True Story of the Mary Celeste" back in 2007. However, this documentary never concluded what happened on that ship all those years ago.

To this day, there has been no closure for anyone on what transpired on that ship. Why did everyone just disappear? Why did the ship itself disappear and then come back?

What happened?

Where is the Mary Celeste Now?

No one knows what happened; no one might ever know what happened on that ship all those years ago. Was it the pirates? The alcohol? The casks? The brothers? The weather? The damaged pipes? The Kraken? The Bermuda Triangle? The aliens? All these questions are valid but will remain unanswered.

What can be answered is this: where is the Mary Celeste now? What is she doing? How is she doing? Is she still haunted? Is she still being used? Or is she in a museum somewhere now? Or being studied in a top-secret facility where people try to regain the missing people? The answers are right here:

After all the commotion towards the Mary Celeste, it had a quiet sail for twelve years. It sailed from place to place, giving different trading items to other ports and being headed by different captains, but it remained haunted.

Though the sailors did not seem to mind, it did not hinder them from voyaging on a boat that had mysteriously ushered people to disappearance. However, just because this ship took a peaceful turn does not mean it took a peaceful end. As much as it is a pain to say, life is not fair to anyone, and now we know it is not fair to anything.

The last captain of the Mary Celeste decided he needed money, so he drowned the ship by means of filling it up with cheap rubber boots and cat food. He made outrageous claims to gain insurance for his "precious" cargo – which just never existed. Unfortunately for the captain, his plan was not all foolproof. You see, the Mary Celeste ran into the Rochelais Reef in Haiti.

The ship may have become a wreckage site, but it refused to sink, allowing the investigators to get a good idea of what happened on the ship and if there was such "precious" cargo the captain was babbling on about, and you know what? They found no such treasure. So now, the Mary Celeste's last action was bringing someone to justice. So you do not think that is poetic?

THE MAN WHO HOPED FOR THE BETTER

"I hope no one would ever break it."

- Poon Lim

On April 5, 1943, just off the coast of Brazil in the Atlantic Ocean, a fishing family spotted a Chinese man drifting on a small raft much smaller than their fishing boat. The man was waving a shirt, jumping up and down, trying to catch their attention, which was a success, seeing as they plucked the man out of his raft and brought him to shore. It took them three days to reach the port of the town of Belen (in Brazil), which was by the Amazon River. The authorities were already waiting for the Chinese man as they figured out who he was. His name is Poon Lim, who survived at sea for 133 days. It was a human record.

Poon Lim was born in Hainan, China, the main island in a group of islands in the South China Sea. Coming from his base, he attended school, which was not normal for the people there, but thanks to his brothers, he could study. At 16, Poon's father was scared of the rising war with the Japanese, so he sent him to live with his brother in the United Kingdom. His brother and Poon got there by being cabin boys on the British Passenger freight train.

According to the book "Sole Survivor" by Ruthanne McCunn, Poon Lim was initially not accustomed to the sea. He would get seasick most of the time and, because of it, was teased by his peers constantly. Eventually, he did learn to be at sea. However, back then, they were not given the ideal treatment. They were discriminated against for their nationality, so they gave them the ugliest jobs on the ship and crammed them into the smallest quarters.

His brother tried to make him feel better by looking at the bright side of things, "at least we are not getting beaten up by the British Officers." He eventually left the place but was in another, maybe even more dire, situation.

This was Poon Lim's life before his adventure took place. He was a cabin boy, made to survive a life given to him because his father thought it would be a better life. And to make matters worse, he had to survive for 133 days on a raft because the ship he was on got bombed by the Nazis. He was the only known survivor.

Surviving out at sea is no easy feat, yet Poon Lim managed to do it for 133 days, even longer than Steven Callahan, who survived for 76 days. What he did was a world record. Even though he did not mean for it to happen, it happened.

The Sinking

When Poon Lim left as a cabin boy, around 1937 and 1938, he moved to Hong Kong, where he studied in a mechanics school. It was not easy during his time, though, since the threats of a Japanese attack were upon them. Then World War 2 came about, and life was even more difficult.

The British people needed more manpower on their ships, and since the discrimination was not as bad and the pay was so much better, Poon Lim joined as a second mess steward on the SS Benlomond, a British merchant ship. The SS Benlomond was also known as the "tramp steamer" because it did not have a set schedule for departure and arrival.

Merchant ships from before were meant to be camouflaged as they carried the country's weapons, such as guns and torpedoes. The British Benlomond was just that, a merchant ship loaded with artillery sailing to Cape Town in South Africa on November 10, 1942.

The main direction of the ship was to Suriname before it went to the United States of America. The protocol when ships crossed the seas back then was to have an accompanying armed forces fleet.

However, for some reason, the SS Benlomond had no such escort because it was a steamer, and steamers do not usually have escorts. The ship contained at least fifty-four people, which included Captain John Maul, Poon Lim, eight gunmen, and forty-four other crew members. The ship may have been armed to the brim with artillery, but it was slow, making it such an easy target when it's time came.

It was November 23, 1942. The SS Benlomond was traveling across the Atlantic Ocean when the hit happened. They were 13 days in, two-thirds of the way to their destination, when the ship was hit by Nazi torpedoes, two to be exact.

The ship started to sink, and it was completely gone in two minutes. Poon Lim, however, grabbed onto a life jacket, which most likely was his saving grace. Poon Lim swam away to survive as the rest of the British and Chinese men drowned and died at the hands of the sea.

He swam as fast as he could away from the sinking SS

Benlomond. Poon Lim swam around the ocean for two hours before finding a raft to hold him up. What kept him afloat was an eight-foot wooden raft that had tins of biscuits, a forty-liter jug of water, chocolate, sugar, two flares, and an electronic torch. It was a stroke of luck, but it was his only luck for some time.

He started to drift along the waters for 133 days, the lone survivor of the SS Benlomond.

Survival While Adrift

Poon Lim called the lift raft he was on "Carley Raft" because that is commonly called a life raft by warships. Truly innovative, Poon Lim used a nail from the raft and wire from the torch to create a fishhook. Then, he used the rope as his fishing line. Because even though the provisions he found were amazing, they will not last long.

So, Poon Lim had to find other ways for him to survive. He used the lid of the can as a knife to cut whatever he could catch on that day. He could catch small fish and even small sharks with the tricks he did, and it kept him alive, but only just. He did not, however, stop at the meat of the sharks. He used the blood of his captured tiny sharks as water to quench his thirst. Specifically, the blood from the shark's liver. He also drank the blood of the birds he was able to catch.

Poon Lim first thought rescue was coming to find him, so he assumed that he would be saved soon because since the SS Benlomond never arrived at the port, people must be searching for it. However, that was not the case. He then realized that no one would dare to cross the waters during a world war. Still, that was not even the saddest part.

The sad part was Poon had so many chances of getting out of the ocean before the 133 days caught up with him. However, since a World War was going on, it was common for the enemy to put up dummy survivors to help ambush those boats. So, at one point, the Americans spotted him, but they did not offer help. The same goes for another time when the Germans spotted him. They did not offer help as well.

They all just thought he was a dummy survivor, a bait for them to get so the "sharks" could ambush them. So, Poon Lim had to endure seasickness, sunburn, and the scarred hope of finding a boat and not being offered any help. He also had to endure the sea's cruel storms upon a small wooden raft.

Storms are always common in the sea. Around the second month of Poon Lim's drifting, he was hit by a storm, almost destroying his raft. Thankfully, it did not. However, it did make him lose all his food and water supplies.

He tied the rope to his wrist and attached it to the boat to survive because he knew he was a terrible swimmer, but he did more than just that. He practiced. He practiced swimming to keep his strength up, and by day 60, he was positive that he could swim by himself.

Poon Lim, however, did his best to keep his sanity. He counted the days by tying knots on the rope he had. Eventually, he stopped making knots and started counting each time the moon would come up. He continued to count until he was rescued.

On April 5, 1943, Poon Lim was spotted by some Brazilian fishermen about 10 miles off the shore of Belem, Brazil. Belem was a town by the mouth of the Amazon River. Due to the difference in language, they could not converse as well as one would hope, but at least Poon Lim could finally eat appropriate food. When he arrived three days after the rescue, he was brought to the hospital, although he was remarkably okay.

He only lost 20 pounds in 133 days and did not need assistance leaving the Brazilian fishermen's boat. He still spent four weeks in the hospital, where he was treated for dehydration and severe sunburn. Once released, he was brought to Britain, where they were all impressed by him surviving for that long and that well. Poon Lim's survival story broke the world record of being adrift at sea.

However, when they said this to him, he hoped no one would have to or want to break it.

> *What's Next? The British Council organized Poon Lim's return to London.*

He became an instant celebrity when he arrived. The story of his survival rang throughout the country, and he was celebrated for his skills. The King then, King George VI, awarded him the British Empire Medal for his courage. The Royal Navy was also impressed by his story of how he used his survival skills. He so inspired them that the techniques he used to survive were written into the Royal Navy's manual.

A reminder for them and himself that he survived and his survival will help the others who find themselves in a similar situation, although he – and everyone else – hopes it would never come to that. After the war, he wished to emigrate to the United States, which he could do despite the challenge. Still, it was possible to do so, thanks to the new legislation written by the Democratic Senator, Walter Magnuson of Washington, back then.

The Democratic Senator granted him citizenship under special consideration. Poon Lim settled in Brooklyn, New York, once he arrived. He lived a peaceful life after that. Well, as peaceful as a celebrity could live. But at least his biggest challenge was done, and he could conquer it to the best of his abilities. People would remember him for his courage and perseverance. And is that not inspiring enough in itself?

Poon Lim lived until January 4, 1991, at the age of 72. Until today, he holds the longest-running record of surviving at sea. As stated earlier, he wishes that no one would ever have to break that record. There is another thing to learn from his story besides the inspiration to survive; the discrimination towards the Chinese from the British back then was no excuse.

Thankfully, in 2006, the British government acknowledged their untoward treatment towards the Chinese during the Second World War, and they established a monumental plaque in honor of the Chinese's contributions to their survival. It stands to this day as a sign of their commitment to not do the wrongs they have committed towards their people ever again.

A COUPLE LOST IS A COUPLE FOUND

"The sea was our life, the animals were our neighbours. I couldn't believe that we were going back to human civilization, and we were wondering what civilization has to offer us now."

– Maurice Bailey.

Maurice and Maralyn Bailey are a British couple who decided to do something very unusual. The premise of their plan to emigrate to New Zealand was not the unusual part, which was very common during that time. The way they were going to New Zealand, though, that was what was unusual about it all. They wanted an adventure by sailing across the ocean for over 14,000 nautical miles in a yacht alone. What makes things even more mind boggling is that they have almost no experience sailing whatsoever. So, is that not something to wonder whether it is a good decision on their end? However, they wanted to do it because they wanted an adventure, and they did get themselves some adventure, do you not think?

Two years have passed since they decided to sell all their belongings and go out to sea. They finally bought a yacht that was 31-foot in size. They named the yacht "Auralyn". They planned to let go and sail across the ocean, not caring about the islands before them and figuring out the islands in front of them, but before we go into their journey, why not take a moment to figure out who these people are? Who are Maurice and Maralyn

Bailey?

Maurice Bailey was born in 1933 in Derbyshire, and according to the interviewer, he did not have the best of upbringings. Sure, he was given a good education, but he did lack in the reception of affection.

He never saw his family again after 19 years old, when he finished his military service. His life did not give him much time to find himself religiously; he renounced anything to do with God. Maralyn Bailey was named Maralyn Collins Harrison in 1941 in Nottingham. At a young age, her parents divorced, and she was then adopted by a Derby couple.

Once she was old enough to work, she worked as a Tax Officer. Maralyn, in contrast to Maurice, actually believes in something. She believes in the supernatural and that how they go to the ocean, drifting and clinging to life, is all predestined. While they were drifting, Maurice almost gave up multiple times, but because of Maralayn's energy, he did not let go. He kept hanging on.

Once they survived and lived their lives, they lived it well. Maralyn died in 2002 due to cancer. The reporter stated that he suspects Maurice has been incredibly lonely since she died. After reading the story and how they cared for each other, you can easily understand why this is so.

Bye, Bye Auralyn

The couple, Maurice and Maralyn Bailey left the shores of their hometown at the beginning of the year 1973. They left Southampton on their Auralyn with not much on them since they sold all their belongings to buy the boat they were already on. They planned to emigrate to New Zealand and build a brand new life there. However, all that youthful hope for a better future drowned, along with the Auralyn.

For some reason, they had confidence that their voyage would be successful and had little to no trouble getting to their destination. This was justified when they could brace through the storms of the sea together somewhat smoothly. This was when they were in the Canary Islands area. Once they reached the Caribbean Sea, they crossed the Panama Channel and broke from their fair travels so far in Panama.

Once ready, they went out to the Galapagos Islands. Which, thankfully for them, was uneventful as well. That is until a sperm whale broke the water's surface and attacked their Auralyn. Because of the force of the "attack," the yacht took significant damage; there was a large hole in the hull just below the water line.

With quick thinking, Maurice tried to cover up the hole with clothes while Maralyn tried to use the water pump. Taking this into account, the couple was not scared of the whale. They felt sorry for it. In one interview, Maurice said, "The poor animal was bleeding extensively from a wound we could not see, and it was close to death." If they had it their way, they might have tried to save the whale from whatever pain it was in. However, that is not what happened.

After everything, Maurice and Maralyn both realized, with dread, that they had to abandon ship. Thankfully, their luck has not run out yet. They had time to inflate their lifeboat and pack food, water, and equipment to help them survive. To be specific, they were able to salvage canned food and water that would last them about 20 days, sextant maps, a compass, two empty buckets, one box of matches, one pair of scissors, binoculars, six emergency flares, and a bag of clothes.

Once everything was onboard the lifeboat, they drifted away from the Auralyn as it slowly sank to the ocean's floor. This happened on March 4, 1973. It was their seventh day out at sea. Well, at least they had six days of good luck, and their seventh day, although unlucky, ended on a bit of a good note because of all the things they were able to salvage and the time they were able to have to get ready on their voyage.

Couples Survival Therapy

Maurice and Maralyn had a crazy idea. According to Maurice's sextant, the couple are about 300 miles northeast of the Galapagos Islands, and the winds were pushing them northwest toward the Pacific. So, they came up with this insane plan of rowing toward safety, toward land, towards civilization again. It does not sound crazy, sure, but the amount of effort you must make to row across oceans manually is great, and the boat is not a rowboat. So, yes, the plan is a bit crazy.

However, they did not give up because they kept on rowing; night and day, they did it. Of course, they took turns, but after three days and three nights, they came to a horrifying realization: they did not move. Due to the increased physical effort, they consumed more daily than they should have. Now, they only have food and water for only five days.

Since they stopped rowing, the winds pushed them toward the northwest. It was a hopeful start since they were being pushed to the shipping lanes that converged along Panama.

However, it was not until eight days of drifting around did they see their first boat, their first hope for a rescue. The couple grabbed a flare gun and shot it, hoping they would be seen, but sadly, they weren't spotted.

They were devastated and even more so that they saw around six other sea vessels over the next months, and still, they weren't spotted. There was even one chance encounter wherein a navy vessel was so close to them, but they had no flare gun at their disposal, so they tried to make a smoke signal. However, the winds were too much, and the vessel kept sailing away.

Although the whole being lost at sea is tragic, some points in their current state were heartwarming to a degree. Why? Because the animals around them seemed to gravitate towards the couple. At first, it was just a bunch of fish, but soon enough, other sea critters came around, such as turtles, dolphins, and sharks.

It was as if their lifeboat became an island of its own, some sort of little ecosystem. In an interview, Maurice said, "We found all animals companionable, and they helped alleviate our isolation." So, in a way, their drifting was not all bad.

Soon enough, they thought of using the animals to their advantage. The couple thought the turtles must have come from somewhere with civilization, so they got some rope, tied their makeshift "island" to the turtles, and allowed them to pull them toward land. However, the plan, albeit brilliant, did not last long because the turtles started to swim in different directions.

As much as they wanted not to harm the animals, they eventually had to survive. So, they took advantage of the birds that came across their path and ate them. Thankfully, the birds did not seem to have any fears when they landed on the lifeboat, so they were easy to catch and eat. Which can't be said the same for turtles because they were very hard to eat due to their shells.

But they were able to eventually not only eat their meat but drink their blood to quench their thirst. Regarding fishing, Maralyn found safety pins they could use as fish hooks (since they had no fish hooks at their disposal). They were also able to catch four sharks. Besides the blood of the turtles they killed, they needed another way to drink, so they would wait for the rain and use the buckets they could salvage to catch it.

So she could continue on this tragic adventure with a positive attitude, Maralyn kept a diary she wrote daily. Her logs became a book on what happened to them in the open seas. It was a catalog of how they survived their situation, proving it could be done.

They were so close to land, actually, by their 45th day. The winds were pushing them northwest, and they were so close.

However, the winds changed, and they drifted away from safety and hope.

The Return

It was their 117th day out at sea, and it started like any normal day of being lost and stranded in the ocean for them. They went over their usual routine until Maralyn told Maurice she could hear a ship's engine. They tried their best to catch its attention but were too weak and tired, so the boat, unsurprisingly, did not see them and kept sailing on, like many of the ships they spotted, but the day did not end there.

On June 30, 1973, a Korean fishing boat found them and brought them home. The boat was called "Weolmi 306," it is usually based at the Tenerife Sea, where it typically fished for tuna. It was later calculated that they drifted for 2400 kilometers before they were rescued.

Once saved, they were brought to Honolulu for medical treatment. They both lost 40 pounds, had trouble walking, obtained ulcers, and suffered from anemia and sunburn. Surprisingly, the couple recovered quickly and immediately went to South Korea, where they showed gratitude to their saviors.

Then, they traveled back to the UK, where they lived in peace. They would reflect on their crazy adventure and how it changed them forever. The couple soon became vegetarians due to their intense dislike for killing. They both wrote a book regarding their time being lost at sea called "117 Days Adrift".

It was revealed in an interview that Maurice felt incredibly lonely after the death of Maralyn in 2002. But he was alright with it, even though he went into isolation after that. Maurice's death was not immediately known.

It was only realized by Alvaro Cerezo, the man's friend and only contact with the outside world, when he stopped receiving letters from Maurice. After some investigation, it was revealed that Maurice had died. He died in 2018.

Alvaro Cerezo was the man who continued telling the story of Maurice and Maralyn Bailey even after both of their deaths. He believed their story should not be forgotten, so he released his interview with Maurice since, unfortunately, he never met

Maralyn. He simply "wanted to do something special for this beautiful couple."

USS INDIANAPOLIS:
THE FINAL VOYAGE

"The ship is safest when it is in port, but that's not what ships are built for."

- Grace Murray Hopper

The life-changing war story of the USS Indianapolis is an interesting 3-in-1 example of triumph, loss, and resilience all weaved into one. During the Second World War, the heavy cruiser played an instrumental role in delivering components for the atomic bomb that would later rock the lives not only of those in the city of Hiroshima and the world. Before it hastened the end of the war with Japan, the Indianapolis took a dark turn after the Japanese submarine I-58 torpedoed the ship in the dead of night on July 30, 1945.

Suffering damage from the Japanese army's torpedoes, the Indianapolis was torn apart in minutes and sank rapidly in the Pacific Ocean. In an instant, the shipwreck left over a thousand of its crew members struggling for survival in the shark-infested waters. When the ordeal began, endurance and resilience were put to the test.

The survivors braved the unforgiving ocean and clung to life for four consecutive excruciating days. Dehydration, exposure, and the sharks roaming around meant that death was just around the corner. While many of them finally succumbed to these extreme conditions, others watched helplessly as sharks dragged their comrades beneath the waves.

A Lockheed PV-1 Ventura patrol bomber spotted the survivors adrift at sea and dropped life rafts for the captain and his men, and one of its crew radioed for help. While the survivors huddled together and waited for search and rescue, the actual rescue operation took too long. As a result, more men perished from the unbearable physical and emotional trauma they experienced while still stranded at sea.

When rescue finally came, only 317 from the original 1,196 crew members were saved, with their story of survival nothing short of a miracle. It became one of the most significant maritime disasters in U.S. naval history that haunted the remaining survivors' lives, their families, and even the victims' families.

The USS Indianapolis shipwreck remains a somber chapter in the annals of history, a stark reminder of the sacrifices made by the brave men who served on board and the atrocities of war. Though fraught with darkness, this true story is also a tale of hope and the indomitable human spirit, proving that even in the face of unimaginable tragedy.

The failure in communication between the Navy Command and Captain Charles B. McVay III's ship became a learning lesson that came at the cost of the lives of men as the tragedy pushed improvements in the reporting of ship positions and the protocols for responding to distress signals. These changes have since been vital in ensuring the safety of naval vessels.

So Far, So Good.

The year is 1945, and the United States of America is at war with Japan in the Second World War. The Naval Headquarters in San Francisco, California, had called the captain of the USS

Indianapolis for his next assignment on the morning of July 15, 1945. All stations on the USS Indianapolis under the command of Captain Charles B. McVay III's command were immediately deployed.

Not much later, two heavily guarded payload crates and accompanying Marines were handed over by two army officers on a military transport aircraft from New Mexico.

McVay was instructed to deliver the top-secret cargo all the way to Tinian as soon as possible. He was prompted that this could end the war faster and prevent any more casualties. While every single second counted, the ship's crew members knew nothing of what the ship was carrying except for a few speculations on what it could be.

Kept in the dark, his crew can only make speculations on whether it was the general's new vehicle or was just cases of liquor for the troops. Little did they know that on board with them were the vital parts that helped create the atomic bomb that would soon wreak havoc on the city of Hiroshima and its people.

Now all aboard on the Indianapolis, the Captain and his crew sailed towards the Mariana Islands on the following day, July 16, 1945. There were neither any escort ships nor contact for the heavy cruiser under the command of McVay. Thus, the Indianapolis cruised smoothly and swiftly in radio silence at a constant speed, going over 30 knots.

The ship made a quick stop over at Pearl Harbor, the Base of Operations for the U.S. Navy, to refuel and proceeded west for Tinian, where McVay and his team of men would safely arrive ten days later (on July 26, 1945). Having unloaded the two unknown crates and the Marines guarding them, the Indianapolis sailed on in completion of the top-secret mission.

While they were heading to Asia, particularly the Philippine Islands, on a regular training mission, McVay regularly communicated with his superiors regarding the whereabouts of the Japanese enemy.

He then requested for some backup in case of some submarine activity in their path. The U.S. Navy had assured McVay that there were no Japanese destroyers in sight and that, as far as the Indianapolis was concerned, it was heavily armed enough to travel safely on its own, with the Japanese forces weakening at the time. Trusting this information from the Navy, the Indianapolis continued at a much conservative pace of 17 knots on the calm seas of the Pacific Ocean.

Where it All Went Wrong

Just when things were beginning to look up for McVay and his team of men, the glory days of the Indianapolis soon ended at the turn of the tide. What seemed to be "mission accomplished" was only the beginning of the final voyage for the heavy cruiser. After the U.S. Navy assured them that there was no enemy threat nearby, McVay decided to change course by no longer zigzagging across the Pacific Ocean.

However, what the U.S. Navy failed to report back to them was the defeat of another of their destroyer ships on the same route (the USS Underhill) just a few days back. The Allied ship faced its tragic demise when a kamikaze plane crash-landed into the warship on July 24, 1945, causing it to explode and sink to the bottom of the ocean. This withheld information would have been the key to saving hundreds of lives in Indianapolis, preventing it from suffering such a similar fate.

Just as the crew was preparing to change shifts at midnight, everything began to unfold on the fateful night of July 29, 1945. Because of the poor visibility, the crew on duty failed to detect the enemy's submarine I-58 patrolling near the Indianapolis. Meanwhile, Lieutenant Commander Hashimoto of the Japanese forces commanded a sneak attack against the Indianapolis, launching a total of six torpedoes underwater.

The attacks were so fast that the American forces didn't have a chance to counterattack, evacuate, or dodge the projectiles. Two out of the six torpedoes caused severe damage to the ship: one near the bow and another mid-ship.

Moments later, the explosions spread fire to the ship and thick black smoke into the air. In just twelve minutes after the first torpedo, the ship tipped over and succumbed to the waves, trapping about three hundred of its men still on deck. In no time, the ship's electrical power had gone out, leaving all of them in pitch-black darkness. The only thing giving them light is the flames eating away the ship.

The Indianapolis was pulled closer to the ocean floor's bottom as minutes passed. Of course, the only logical way to survive the wreck is to swim, and so the sailors offloaded themselves out into the ocean with or without life vests. On the other hand, those in the radio rooms attempted to give out distress signals. Unfortunately, all their communication systems had died. This would only mean that McVay and the remainder of his men of about nine hundred sailors were stranded at sea.

The fate of the Indianapolis was a cry for help but with no sound. Having assumed that the ship had always traveled in radio silence from the start of the mission, the U.S.

Navy did not know right away of the endangered state of the ship as they did not receive any distress signal on their end.

In addition to this, the shipwreck was situated so far away from the trade routes that there was little to no chance for the survivors to be noticed by a vessel that could have come to their aid. Because of this, no one from the U.S. Navy who was in the Philippines expected them, so no search attempts were immediately made.

At this point, death was just around the corner for the surviving men of the Indianapolis. About fifty of them had passed away the next morning due to injuries. The smell of blood from the wounded, dead, and living crew attracted sharks in the ocean. The group of survivors gave their best effort to prevent the shark attacks against their own kind.

Still, with no search and rescue for the men aboard the Indianapolis, they faced more challenges, such as hunger, dehydration, hallucination, and drowning due to panic or natural causes.

With only less than half of the survivors left, one could say the men on the Indianapolis were done for (especially with the ship three days gone and their life vests completely sad and useless). Still, it was not until an aircraft passing by sighted them and radioed their coordinates.

The Aftermath

About four days after the attack, a passerby Lockheed PV-1 Ventura patrol bomber flew across the Pacific Ocean when they noticed the men floating in the sea. They immediately reported the sighting and a rescue operation was launched on August 2, 1945.

Multiple ships and an aircraft were dispatched to the shipwreck site, where the remaining survivors hung on to their lives on the rafts.

The number of sharks swarming the location made rescue efforts more challenging. Before the rescue team arrived, several men had already died. Thus reducing the number of survivors. By the time the rescue was completed, only 316 of the USS Indianapolis's original 1,196 crew members had survived.

While the loss of the Indianapolis was a significant setback for the U.S. Navy, the mission it had just completed changed the world. The components it delivered ultimately led to the atomic bombing of two Japanese cities: Hiroshima on August 6, 1945, and Nagasaki on August 9, 1945.

It marked the first and only use of nuclear weapons in the Second World War. The devastating power of these bombs played a pivotal role in bringing Japan to a defeat and, finally, ending the Second World War.

In contrast, though significant, the sinking of the Indianapolis is not common knowledge to the public due to the overpowering events that happened after. The ship's tragic loss occurred amid numerous other wartime tragedies, and it was only tangentially related to the atomic bomb's delivery.

Nevertheless, both events underscore the complex and often devastating consequences of war, with the atomic bombing of Hiroshima taking center stage as a turning point in history. At the same time, the Indianapolis sinking remains a poignant reminder of the many sacrifices made during the Second World War.

The atomic bombing attacks of Hiroshima and Nagasaki had far-reaching and long-lasting consequences. While they hastened the end of the war, they also raised ethical, moral, and geopolitical questions about the use of nuclear weapons. The aftermath of these bombings spurred discussions about the necessity of arms control, non-proliferation agreements, and the potential for future conflict.

Meanwhile, ship commander McVay faced a court-martial for the loss of the ship. He was found guilty of hazarding his ship by failing to zigzag to dodge the torpedoes. A decision later deemed controversial because the information on the ship's location had not reached him in time.

McVay was posthumously pardoned by U.S. Congress, recognizing the unjust decision of his court-martial in 2000. The events surrounding the sinking and the atomic bombings underscore the profound impact and legacy of the Second World War, which continues to shape global politics and international relations today.

OUTRUNNING DEATH:
THE LOUIS ZAMPERINI STORY

"The choice is not between violence and nonviolence but between nonviolence and nonexistence."

— *Martin Luther King Jr.*

Another harrowing tale of survival against all odds that showcased human resilience and determination in the face of unimaginable adversity is the remarkable shipwreck experience of Louis Zamperini. Louis Silvie Zamperini, born in 1917, was an American Olympic distance runner and a veteran of the Second World War. His shipwreck story began in his days in the U.S. Army Air Forces, where he was a bombardier.

In May 1943, his plane crashed into the Pacific Ocean while doing a search and rescue mission. He and two other crew members, Russell Allen Phillips and Francis McNamara, survived the crash. They found themselves adrift on a small life raft in the vast expanse of the Pacific.

Extreme physical and psychological challenges marked their ordeal. They survived on meager rations and rainwater while battling intense exposure to harsh environments such as the scorching sun, the frigid nights, and the constant threat of sharks tested their resolve. They also had to contend with the relentless psychological strain of being stranded in the open ocean without knowing if they would ever be rescued.

One of the most harrowing aspects of their journey was the persistent and terrifying presence of sharks. Zamperini later recounted how the sharks regularly ram the life raft, hoping to topple it and get to the men inside. The constant fear of shark attacks was a nightmarish reality they had to endure. They also captured and killed birds and fish to sustain themselves but were often left with guilt over taking life to preserve their own.

Hope was waning as weeks turned into months. They drifted thousands of miles in the open sea, where they were initially believed to be lost. They clung to life with an unwavering will to survive the situation. They spoke of their families, shared stories, and provided mutual emotional support for each other.

Rescue came after forty-seven days of despair when a Japanese patrol plane found them. Unfortunately, the Japanese captured them, marking the end of their dangerous shipwreck but the start of new hardships as prisoners of war (POW).

His tale of survival in the shipwreck and his subsequent internment in Japanese POW camps is recounted in Laura Hillenbrand's "Unbroken" and a film adaptation by Angelina Jolie. His resilience and unyielding spirit became a testament to the human will in the face of insurmountable adversity.

After his release, Zamperini returned to the United States, forgave his captors, and worked to inspire others with his remarkable story.

His shipwreck and the following trials serve as a powerful reminder of the human spirit's strength and ability to overcome even the harshest challenges.

His legacy inspires people worldwide, underscoring the

enduring human spirit's capacity to persevere despite their circumstances.

Early Beginnings

Louis Zamperini's early life was a primer to his determination in adversity. He was the son of Italian immigrants, and his family moved to Torrance in California when he was just a child. Growing up, he faced significant challenges due to his limited English language skills and the discrimination faced by Italian immigrants during that era. He endured bullying and prejudice but quickly overcame these obstacles through his tenacity and determination.

One of the turning points in Zamperini's life was his discovery of running. He initially channeled his energy and competitive spirit into the sport to escape bullies. His natural talent for running soon became evident, and he quickly rose to prominence as a high school track star, earning the nickname "Torrance Tornado" for his blazing speed.

Louis Zamperini's athletic prowess earned him a scholarship to the University of Southern California (USC), where he further honed his running skills. He set collegiate records at USC and became a track and field sensation. His signature race was the mile run, and his exceptional finishing kick in the final lap was a source of awe and inspiration.

In 1936, Zamperini represented the United States at the Berlin Olympics. He competed in the 5,000-meter race and finished in eighth place. His remarkable performance caught the attention of Adolf Hitler, who requested a personal meeting with the young athlete—this moment marked one of the high points of Zamperini's early life and his burgeoning athletic career.

However, the outbreak of the Second World War dramatically altered the course of Zamperini's life. He enlisted in the United States Army Air Forces as a B-24 Liberator bomber bombardier and served in the Pacific theater. During his military service, he experienced pivotal life events that later molded him into a symbol of resilience and survival.

Before embarking on his ill-fated mission in the war, Zamperini became part of a close-knit crew in the United States Army Air Forces, where he met their aircraft pilot, Lieutenant Russell Allen Phillips, who became one of his best comrades. His leadership was crucial, and the trust between the pilot and the bombardier was paramount.

Another integral member of their team was the tail gunner, Francis McNamara. McNamara was responsible for operating the tail gun, a vital position for the defense of the aircraft. He shared the same sense of duty and commitment to their mission as Zamperini's fellow crew members.

The crew's bonds extended beyond their professional roles. They shared the challenges, fears, and hopes that come with military service during a time of war. With families and dreams waiting for them back home, their shared experiences created a unique and unbreakable camaraderie that helped them power through what would happen next.

Tough Luck

Like his athletic career, Zamperini blazed through the ranks as a Second Lieutenant during his bombardier days in the Second World War. He and his team pulled off a dangerous yet successful raid with his crew on the Japanese-held island of Nauru, where he and his comrades fought against three Japanese Zero warplanes.

While it was remarkable that they shot over five hundred holes into the enemy's ship, it still came at an expense after losing a crew member. Fortunately, Zamperini was able to help save the lives of four other men who got wounded in the assault.

Soon after the mission, he and his crew got reassigned to another bomber plane named "The Green Hornet." The Green Hornet was said to have had a history of mechanical difficulties, including rumbles around its base. However, after running diagnostics, the plane was declared "good to go."

The aircraft embarked on a search-and-rescue mission conducted by Zamperini and his comrades on May 27, 1943. The primary objective of their mission was simple: retrieve their missing airmen and safely return to the base. While this all sounded simple, the task was inherently dangerous, as it required long flights over the Pacific Ocean, a region notorious for its vastness and the looming threat of enemy encounters.

The rescue mission suddenly became the most pivotal and harrowing experience. After flying over eight hundred miles from Hawaii, Zamperini's bomber plane suddenly faced mechanical difficulties until its fateful emergency crash landing into open waters despite the crew's collective efforts to regain control.

The impact of the crash in the water was violent and disorienting. All eleven men aboard were declared missing in action. After a year, still with no sign of them, they were assumed killed in activity among the many other war heroes who died in the Second World War.

Eight from the original headcount deployed on the Green Hornet died during the crash, leaving only Francis McNamara, Russell Allen Phillips, and Louis Zamperini alive. Fortunately, the three survivors managed to get away from the wreckage on emergency rafts. While they had survived the crash, their plight had only just begun.

It was an uphill battle. Though surrounded by water, they had almost no food and potable water. Desperate to survive, the trio harvested rainwater instead of saltwater, which would have caused them to dehydrate more quickly. For food, they caught small fish and birds on their raft. They even strategized their survival methods using the birds as bait to catch more fish.

More dangers awaited them at sea, and trials soon tested the limits of each one. Though things became more heated when McNamara desperately ate their tiny supply of chocolate, he later redeemed himself by grabbing an oar to fend off a massive shark during an attack. Phillips and Zamperini would only have made it alive later on with him.

Aside from storms, it would rain bullets from the Japanese warplanes that would strafe their raft and barely miss them. McNamara was the first to give out thirty-three days later, as his body could only take so much. In return, his two comrades wrapped his body in whatever they had available and pushed his corpse overboard as an informal but solemn funeral at sea.

With that, the Green Hornet's crew was down to two. On their forty-seventh day, with no rescue, the two survivors washed ashore on an island. They finally saw signs of human life, which wasn't necessarily a good sign as that territory was under Japanese rule.

The Japanese soldiers on the Marshall Islands took the two American soldiers under their custody, holding them captive, physically beating them with wooden clubs, and interrogating them until they moved to the Ofuna camp in Japan a month later.

Technically, they weren't classified as POWs because the Japanese army didn't transfer them to regular camps for captives. Instead, they were promoted to a higher facility for super maximum level inmates for pilots and submarine officers who were well-versed with military technology. Zamperini experienced a year of physical, emotional, and psychological hardships under his captors until he transferred to two other camps: Omori and his last destination, Naoetsu.

Trial by Fire

Towards the war's end, Zamperini endured a harrowing odyssey, shuttling from one Japanese prison camp to another. Starvation became his grim companion, so much so that he resorted to eating rice off the prison floor after Japanese officials callously flung it at him. Zamperini's notoriety as an Olympic hero made him a focal point for his captors.

One man, an anti-American propagandist named James Sasaki, even confronted him. Sasaki, a former schoolmate, challenged Zamperini to races against well-fed Japanese runners despite his emaciated condition.

But the most brutal of his tormentors was Sergeant Matsuhiro Watanabe, infamously known as "The Bird." Throughout his time at the Ofuna prison camp, Zamperini was subjected to repeated and vicious beatings at the hands of The Bird as a form of punishment.

One pivotal moment came when Zamperini, in an attempt to retain a semblance of dignity, agreed to deliver a propaganda message denouncing the United States' war efforts but insisted on crafting the script himself. This shocking revelation confounded his family, who had been informed of his death and posthumously awarded him the Purple Heart.

When Sasaki demanded that Zamperini read a second propaganda script written by the Japanese, Zamperini refused.

The Bird infuriated, ordered the other inmates to assault him viciously. This horrifying ordeal fanned the flames of Zamperini's desire for revenge against his tormentors, though The Bird would ultimately be promoted to a higher position at Naoetsu camp.

The conditions within these camps were nothing short of deplorable, marked by squalor and trauma, but this grim chapter would eventually yield Zamperini's return to freedom.

In August 1945, Japan finally surrendered to the United States, ending over two years of captivity for Zamperini and his fellow POWs. The arrival of American B-29 bombers signified liberation, forcing the Japanese military to shut down their prisoner camps, including Naoetsu, where Zamperini was held. For Zamperini, it meant one thing and everything: he was coming home.

His return home was bittersweet as he grappled with the traumas of war. Though reunited with his family, the weight of survivor's guilt, nightmares, and post-traumatic stress loomed heavily. Despite these challenges, Zamperini sought healing through love and faith.

Amidst the tumultuous post-war period, Zamperini chose to rebuild his life. A year after liberation, he married Cynthia Applewhite in 1946. He found solace in evangelical Christianity after attending a life-changing Billy Graham Crusade in 1949 to confront his war-induced pain and salvage his marriage.

Zamperini's extraordinary journey of evading death left an indelible mark on him. In a remarkable twist, he forgave his captors and became a staunch advocate for peace. His 2003 memoir, "Devil at My Heels," was a testament to his survival, resilience, and gratitude.

THE ESSEX:
A WHALING TRAGEDY

"There is, one knows not what sweet mystery about this sea, whose gently awful stirrings seem to speak of some hidden soul beneath..."

— *Herman Melville, Moby-Dick*

The Essex is an 87-foot whaling ship that sailed from Nantucket, Massachusetts, in 1819. Its story of resilience and suffering came at the expense of unimaginable adversity, as it is based on horrifying real-life events faced by Captain George Pollard Jr. and his crew in their voyage at sea. At the time, the Essex set out to hunt for oil. It was not just any oil, but the oil harvested from the fat of sperm whales.

Sperm oil quickly became a commodity in the 19th century because of its many valuable uses. For example, it can produce high-quality bright flames that are ideal for oil lamps and lighthouses, as it produces little soot and smoke. It was also used as a lubricant for machines in the Industrial Revolution due to its low viscosity, which allowed the machinery to run smoothly.

Aside from industrial applications, it also had medicinal value as it was used topically in soaps and cosmetics. The other redeeming properties of sperm oil are its quality and longevity because it can remain in a liquid state at different temperatures than other types of oil. Profit became the driving force for expeditions like the Essex's for the crew, the shipping company, and the economy.

The Essex's expedition began with a series of unfortunate events from the get-go. Just after the ship set sail, a storm had already caused some damage to the vessel, which tested their resolve. This decision led them to Cape Horn after five challenging weeks. Their troubles persisted even more when the overfished whaling grounds led them astray toward a more remote area in the South Pacific.

This was followed by another casualty when they reached the Galapagos Islands when the crew members of the Essex encountered and decided to collect tortoises. After horsing around, a fire broke, inviting even more bad luck in their ill-fated voyage.

Finally, when the Essex came across a pod of whales, the men on the ship took out their whaleboats and harpooned the mammals back into the ship. One whale even tugged against one of the whaleboats. This coined the term "Nantucket sleighride". While it seems that the Essex found her lot, her glory days were soon over.

An enormous sperm whale, more massive than the Essex, rampaged and wrecked the ship. This turn of events caused the ship to sink, leaving only eight out of over twenty crew members who made do on only three leaking whaleboats and cannibalism with no food and drinkable water. This open sea ordeal would go on for 90 days at sea until their rescue in February 1421. The tragic events following the Essex are memorialized in Herman Melville's literary classic, "Moby Dick."

The Whale Expedition

Before embarking on its ill-fated journey, the Essex was a prominent and iconic whaling ship that spanned 87 feet long. It was built from durable white oak in Amesbury, Massachusetts. In 1799, it was used for commerce as a merchant vessel before being stationed in Nantucket, the hometown of American whaling.

During the early 19th century, whaling became a challenging trade that required finding whales in 25-foot-long boats, usually in groups of six crew members. The crew would harpoon the whale, securing it to their boat with a rope.

After taming the whale, they would use a lance on it, and the hunt would soon end. Then, they would tow their catch to the main ship and extract the oil from the blubber of the sperm whales. The Essex became well-renowned as a whaler because of this.

The pursuit of extracting sperm whales commenced right away in August 1819 under the leadership of Captain George Pollard Jr. until its demise two and a half years later. The nightmarish ordeal would begin on the first two days at sea.

A powerful storm struck the Essex days after it left the harbor. The storm was so strong that it destroyed its topgallant sail. It was the first instance that the Essex almost sank. Fortunately, all twenty-one voyagers arrived in Cape Horn five weeks after their first near-death experience.

The crew sailed on. Upon reaching the overexploited whaling grounds of South America, they decided to head to another whaling area farther down the South Pacific.

Briefly, the sailors anchored at Charles Island in the Galapagos. On their way there, the crew toyed around and collected tortoises. However, such carelessness caused a fire that almost claimed the lives of the men.

This event foreshadowed the rest of their time aboard.

Fast forward to November 1820, Pollard's crew conducted successful extractions over the past months, wherein he and his crew on the Essex made the "Nantucket sleigh ride" a thing from harpooning the whales.

However, the Essex's heyday ended when Owen Chase, one of Pollard's men, supervised the ship repairs and saw something he shouldn't have.

Alas, it was an enormous 85-foot whale. At first, it seemed like the whale was only peacefully floating by, but life flashed before the crew's eyes when the giant whale charged toward the ship head-on and struck the Essex at such rapidity in agitation.

The turbulence almost tossed everyone aboard overboard. In disbelief of what happened, the crew members were unprepared for the whale's surprise attack. The mammal was so distressed and furious at its extortionists that the impact from the collision caused the ship major damage. The Essex had only two choices: to sink or to float.

Abandon Ship

Having its much-awaited revenge, the culprit had vanished in plain sight a few moments before the sinking of the Essex. Meanwhile, the crew tried to attend to the shipwreck in its last moments.

However, their efforts were no match for the whale's return. The whale raced towards the ship, twice as fast as before this time, and struck a direct blow to the ship's bow, then left for good.

Water started seeping rapidly below deck. In a split second, the crew members had no choice but to evacuate the ship using the smaller boats as a last resort to ensure their survival. They tried to bring essentials such as navigation, bread, water, and supplies before the Essex finally capsized.

Pollard, who had just returned from whaling in another boat, returned to find the Essex in a hopeless situation. In disbelief, he asked Chase to explain what happened. Chase told his captain that a whale had overturned the ship. The others returned, and all of them fell silent in devastation.

At first, the men hesitated to "abandon ship." After assessing the dire situation, they maximized their resources, including three tiny boats for the twenty men. LOst at sea, they headed towards the nearest land according to their calculations.

Considering the wind direction, they had only two options: the Marquesas Islands, 1,200 miles away, and the Society Islands, 2,000 miles away. Two of Pollard's mates, Chase and Matthew Joy, argued to head towards Peru and Chile because they might come across cannibals in the nearby islands.

However, the two South American countries were 4,000 miles away. Another reason why they didn't go for it was because of where the wind blew and the strong current.

The men were divided among the three makeshift whaleboats for the next two months under the lead and command of Pollard, Chase, and Joy. Their provisions later dwindled as dehydration eventually set in, and their boats needed repairs occasionally. Pollard's boat gave out first after suffering from an attack by a killer whale towards the end of that year.

By the last month of the year 1820, they covered over 1,500 miles and arrived at what they assumed to be Ducie Island. They arrived at a different island nearby that was named Henderson. On the island, they found fresh water but not food.

After consulting their charts and assessing their situation, the remaining survivors continued their journey. Instead of going to Chile, they headed towards Easter Island for practical reasons. The first option was distanced at 3,000 miles, while the latter was much closer, within a range of 1,000 miles.

On Henderson, three men chose to stay behind on the lonely island.

On January 10, 1821, Joy became the first sailor to pass away on the Essex. The men buried his body at sea. Obed Hendricks took over his command as the boat's captain in his passing.

The men of the Essex began dying one by one. Just a day after Joy's death, a storm followed, leading Chase's boat astray. One of his men passed away over a week later.

Weeks later, another sailor in Chase's boat died, but this time, the other sailors resorted to cannibalism to stay alive.

Fortunately, the last three sailors in Chase's boat came across a nearby ship and managed to sail toward it. The three men survived eighty-nine days at sea.

While the others' ordeal had ended, the other whaleboats faced grimmer circumstances that January. Three men died on Hendricks' boat and were eaten for the others' survival. Similarly, Pollard lost a crew member who shared a similar fate.

The two vessels went different ways the next day. The fate of the boat carrying Hendricks and two others, none of whom had navigational equipment, remains unknown. However, a whaleboat with three skeletons was discovered later on Ducie Island, speculated to have come from the Essex.

On the other hand, Pollard went to great lengths, such as drawing lots to determine who would be eaten next. Finally, on February 23, 1821, only two men from the Essex crew on Pollard's boat made it alive. American sailors rescued them on Dauphin, another whaling ship.

Life and Fiction

All those rescued from the Essex tragedy were transported to Valparaíso, Chile, where the survivors reunited. Upon learning about the men stranded on Ducie Island, the Australian ship Surry was dispatched to their aid.

However, after finding no one on Ducie Island, the Surry sailed to Henderson Island, where, on April 9, 1821, it successfully rescued the remaining survivors.

For Chase, upon their return to Nantucket, he penned an account of the extraordinary and distressing shipwreck, originally called the "Narrative of the Most Extraordinary and

Distressing Shipwreck of the Whale-ship Essex" in 1821, which was subsequently republished under various titles.

Another survivor, Thomas Nickerson, who served as a former cabin boy on the Essex, came up with his narrative of the ship's sinking and the subsequent rescue later on. Unfortunately, his notebook was lost and remained unpublished until 1984.

Chase's work later served as the true story that inspired Herman Melville's classic novel, "Moby Dick," in 1851, thirty years after the maritime tragedy happened. "Moby Dick," while inspired by those real-life events, is a work of fiction, and not a historically accurate account of the Essex incident, as he took significant creative liberties in crafting his novel.

While the literary work featured a vengeful white sperm whale, Moby Dick, the events and characters are primarily products of Melville's imagination in a rich and symbolic narrative that delved into themes of obsession, revenge, and the human condition.

On the other hand, the real-life story of the Essex has inspired other contemporary books, films, and film adaptations based on the concept of doomed whaleship people stranded at sea.

The sinking of the Essex also served as one of the contributing factors to the decline of the whaling industry. Along with similar incidents, it sheds light on whalers' immense risks and challenges. These stories, coupled with an endangered whale population due to overhunting, raised awareness about the importance of conservation.

By the mid-19th century, alternative sources of oil, such as petroleum, eventually replaced whale oil for lighting and lubrication, diminishing the economic viability of whaling. Additionally, the rise of environmental and conservation movements in the 20th century led to stricter regulations and, eventually, the prohibition of commercial whaling.

The establishment of the International Whaling Commission (IWC) in 1946 aimed to oversee whaling practices and protect whale species. Over time, the IWC implemented bans on commercial whaling, influenced by the declining whaling industry, of which the Essex story was a part.

While the sinking of the Essex didn't directly cause the whaling ban, it contributed to changing public perceptions. It played a role in the whaling industry's decline and the emergence of conservation efforts.

MEET THE ROBERTSONS:
THE FAMILY AT SEA

"Our most basic instinct is not for survival but for family."

—Paul Pearsall

The Robertson family's shipwreck story is a remarkable tale of survival against the odds. Their journey was supposed to be a sailing adventure, but it soon became harrowing. It began in 1971 when the family of six embarked on a voyage across the Pacific Ocean. The Robertsons consisted of Dougal and Lyn Robertson, the parents, plus their four children: son Douglas, aged 17, daughter Anne, aged 16, and twins Neil and Sandy, aged 9.

Aboard their 43-foot schooner named "Lucette," the family initially planned to sail to the Mediterranean through the Panama Canal, a journey that would take them across the vast Pacific Ocean. Their voyage went smoothly at first, as they enjoyed the freedom and adventure of life at sea. However, their luck would run out eventually as the trip began to take a drastic turn for the worse when they encountered a fierce storm in the South Pacific. The storm battered their vessel, causing severe damage and forcing them to abandon it.

On June 15, 1972, the Lucette was struck suddenly by a pod of killer whales, which caused extensive damage to the hull. With their boat rapidly taking on water, the Robertsons had no choice but to evacuate to a life raft they would name the "Ednamair." They salvaged what supplies they could, which included some canned food, a small amount of freshwater, and a makeshift sail.

The family of five found themselves drifting across the vastness of the Pacific Ocean, miles and miles away from the nearest land. Their situation was dire, as they faced the challenges of survival at sea. They had to ration their limited supplies and find ways to catch fish for sustenance. In addition to the physical hardships, the psychological toll of being stranded in the open ocean took its toll on the family.

The Robertsons' ordeal lasted for an astonishing 38 days, during which they drifted in the vast Pacific. They faced the constant threat of dehydration, exposure to the elements, and the uncertainty of their fate. However, they didn't lose hope and determination throughout this time and did their best to survive.

On July 23, 1972, the Japanese finally rescued the Robertsons after enduring their journey on the Ednamair. Fortunately, a Japanese vessel, the Toka Maru II, was en route to the Panama Canal when its crew spotted their distress signal and took good care of them. They even let the family bring their empty dinghy with them onboard to remember their family adventure (or rather, misadventure).

Meanwhile, on land, the global media awaited the family's arrival. The Robertsons safely arrived in Panama on July 28, 1972,

From Farm To Vessel

A family of six lived in an English village called Meerbrook. The Robertson family comprised Dougal, the 47-year-old father; Lyn, the mother; and their four children: 17-year-old Douglas, 16-year-old Anne, and twins Neil and Sandy, at the ripe age of 9. The family traded their life on a small dairy farm for an adventure of a lifetime in 1971.

It all began when Neil, the family's youngest child, fell in love with the idea of circumnavigating the globe without stopping. It was an idea introduced to him by a bedtime story about Robin Knox-Johnston.

The whole family would later entertain this suggestion as they embarked on a similar maritime exploration. Though initially hesitant, Dougal, their father, soon considered the potential of this daring adventure.

While it served as an excellent opportunity for his children to see the world waiting outside their farm, he decided for all of them to go because their family was facing financial struggles. At the time, their dairy farm teetered on the brink of bankruptcy.

In 1971, Dougal decided to sell the farm and used his family's life savings to buy a 43-foot wooden schooner. They named the trusty 50-year-old vessel Lucette.

Though the boat had repairs in the past, the father betted on it and believed that Lucette had a fighting chance against the odds in their circumnavigation. Soon, the family left their hometown and traveled to Falmouth in southwestern England, where Lucette awaited them.

This grand adventure marked the family's first sailing experience together primarily because they had no experience before this journey began except for Dougal, a former marine who brought his expertise to navigate Lucette.

Initially, they wanted to sail across the Atlantic Ocean,

through the Panama Canal, then across the globe. Remarkably, they embarked on this audacious journey without prior practice or training. They plunged headfirst into the open sea rather than conducting a trial sail in nearby waters.

Soon, the Robertsons navigated across the Atlantic, enduring heavy rains at sea. The Caribbean Islands served as their stopovers to replenish their food supplies.

After the Panama Canal, their adventure led them to the captivating Galapagos Islands, known for their volcanic formations, unique sands, and remarkable wildlife. However, things eventually took a tragic turn after they departed the Galapagos.

On June 15, 1972, they encountered a pod of killer whales. What started as a seemingly innocent encounter rapidly turned menacing. The orcas began to attack their boat relentlessly, causing severe damage and leaving them no option but to abandon the ship.

Amid the chaos, they boarded an inflatable raft and a long dinghy, taking with them only the essentials. Lucette sank in less than a minute, leaving them adrift in the Pacific Ocean.

Lost at Sea

After Lucette disappeared beneath the waves, they only had enough water for ten days and emergency rations for three days on the raft. Lyn had taken their papers, the logbook, and a bag of onions with her in addition to a kitchen knife, a tin of biscuits, some fruits, a pound of sweets, and flares.

Aside from this, she had also brought her sewing box, which

was handy as they had no maps, compasses, or instruments, and nobody knew they were missing. Their fight for survival had begun.

Their challenges were just beginning as they faced dehydration and the harsh realities of survival. Deprived of a radio and with limited rations, they knew the clock was ticking. The lifeboats were tied together with a wire rope.

They initially planned to sail back to the Galapagos Islands, hoping for a rescue, but they soon realized the strong current was against them. Instead, they decided to brave the Doldrums, a region near the equator known for its low winds and weak ocean currents—a nightmare for sailors but perfect for their small lifeboats.

Dehydration loomed as their most pressing challenge. Despite being surrounded by water, the ocean's salt content rendered it undrinkable.

They relied on collecting rainwater to stay hydrated, taking calculated risks to capture it during frequent thunderstorms. Their makeshift survival kit included nine liters of water, flares, a first aid kit, a fishing kit, a mirror, a knife, anchors, paddles, and wooden bellows to keep the inflatable raft afloat.

The sun and limited rations took a toll in their first week adrift. Their food supplies rapidly dwindled, and they resorted to consuming raw sea creatures, including sea turtles.

They hunted these creatures using their bare hands and improvised tools, drinking their blood and utilizing their fat as a makeshift skin ointment.

Dried fish became their primary source of sustenance, although they encountered another challenge on the 14th day when the inflatable raft began to leak. With no hope of repairing it, they reluctantly abandoned it and crammed into the long dinghy, leaving their possessions behind.

Now confined to a small space, their legs grew sore, and they feared standing up for the risk of capsizing the dinghy. Dougal and Lyn kept a constant vigil at night to prevent their children from accidentally falling overboard while asleep.

They sang songs and shared stories to maintain their spirits, providing much-needed moments of relief and hope.

Throughout their ordeal, they recorded details of each day in an improvised logbook using a biro from Lyn's sewing box. The days continued to bring challenges and small victories as the family struggled for survival. They caught turtles, relied on enemas to absorb water, weathered storms, and faced the constant threat of dehydration.

More challenges ensued, such as the dinghy breaking away from the raft, wherein Dougal had to swim to retrieve it, narrowly escaping sharks. They were also in bad shape after developing sores, boils, and sunburn despite the continuous rain.

At some point, the Robertsons had no choice but to transfer to the dinghy, as the bottom of the raft was virtually gone. They salvaged as much as possible from the raft, including flotation pieces and a canopy for shelter, but movement was limited, making it almost impossible to keel.

After thirty-eight days adrift at sea, Dougal saw a distant boat on the horizon. Seizing this opportunity, he ignited the flare he had conserved and hoped for the boat's notice. The flare emitted light for a minute before extinguishing.

Initially, the distant boat showed no sign of acknowledgment, leading the family to believe that their emergency flare had gone unnoticed.

However, five minutes later, the boat's bow gradually turned and aimed toward them. They were then rescued by a Japanese fishing vessel en route to the Panama Canal.

The family was severely dehydrated and had shed a substantial amount of weight. The compassionate fishermen provided them with food until they reached land and were subsequently rushed to the hospital for a thorough checkup.

The long dinghy that saved them was later donated. It is now exhibited at the National Maritime Museum in Falmouth, England, a valuable remembrance of their family's attempt to circumnavigate the world.

Homecoming

The Ednamair played a pivotal role in their survival and the family's story of resilience and unwavering determination that would later garner global attention. To memorialize the unforgettable family's voyage at sea, the National Maritime Museum Cornwall in Falmouth took Robertson's dinghy as a display in its permanent exhibit.

Its presence in the museum holds great historical significance due to its close association with the incredible survival saga of the Robertson family as the family's lifeline during their 38-day ordeal at sea after their sailboat, the Lucette, was attacked and sunk by killer whales.

The Ednamair took its name from Lyn Robertson's sisters, Edna and Mary. It was named after them after her sister Edna generously provided the funds for the family to purchase the dinghy.

Even after the family's rescue in 1972, the Ednamair was initially cared for by Edna until its relocation back to Falmouth, the birthplace of the Robertson family's voyage, and eventual donation to the National Maritime Museum Cornwall.

Other related artifacts and mementos that joined the display at the museum are teeth from a 5-foot Mako shark, Lyn's pressure cooker weight that also served as a fishing weight, some turtle oil, and an enema tube. The turtle's oil was valuable to the family because it played an instrumental role in the survival of the Robertsons.

The family produced it by melting turtle fat in the sun. It served different applications, from topical remedies that helped them alleviate saltwater boils and keep themselves warm to being used in stew with fish and turtle meat. Aside from these, it also was used as an enema.

On the other hand, the enema tube was ingeniously crafted from the life raft's boarding ladder. The family used it to rehydrate themselves with only the stagnant water from the bottom of the boat.

By exhibiting what remains of the Robertson family's possessions at sea, the museum fulfills the vital role of preserving and sharing this inspirational tale with the public, allowing visitors to immerse themselves in the history and the extraordinary journey of the Robertsons.

To this day, the Robertson family's survival narrative remains a testament to human endurance and ingenuity that continues to inspire and captivate people. The museum commemorated the 50th anniversary of this extraordinary tale of human resilience with a dialogue by one of the Robertson children, Douglas Robertson himself.

During his talk, he recalled from personal experience all the events that transpired at sea from June 15, 1972, and the next 38 days in their fight for survival.

Meanwhile, his father, Dougal Robertson, published a book called "Survive the Savage Sea," which also recounted their family's remarkable survival journey that would gain widespread success later on.

THE EXPEDITION OF ALL EXPEDITIONS: THOR HEYERDAHL AND THE KON-TIKI

"Fear not the unknown. It is a sea of possibilities."

– Tom Althouse

The Norwegian explorer and ethnographer Thor Heyerdahl was an internationally renowned figure known for the Kon-Tiki Expedition of 1947. During this, he crossed the Pacific Ocean on a raft made of balsa wood to substantiate his theory about ancient South American interactions with Polynesia. Heyerdahl's adventures and writings expanded the worldview of ancient maritime activities and the spread of cultures, contributing to the body of knowledge, particularly in the distinct fields of seafaring and anthropology.

The expedition's primary objective was to provide evidence that ancient South Americans could have settled in the remote Polynesian islands using simple navigation and transportation methods. This theory contradicted the widely accepted belief that Polynesians had originated in Southeast Asia and migrated to the Pacific islands.

Inspired by the similarities he observed between Polynesian and South American cultures, particularly in language, folklore, and archaeological discoveries, he hypothesized that the ancient South American communities had crossed the Pacific Ocean on rafts made of balsa wood and other natural materials.

Determined to test his theory, the explorer and his crew constructed the Kon-Tiki, a raft comprising nine large balsa logs and a bamboo framework. The raft design was based on the kind of vessels that, according to Heyerdahl's theory, South Americans might have used to reach Polynesia.

On April 28, 1947, the Kon-Tiki expedition set sail from the port of Callao in Peru, embarking on a challenging 4,300-mile journey across the Pacific Ocean.

The voyage encountered numerous difficulties, including strong currents, turbulent seas, shark encounters, and equipment malfunctions. The crew relied on basic navigation methods, such as celestial observations and dead reckoning, to plot their course.

After a hundred days at sea, the Kon-Tiki eventually reached the shore, resting on the Raroia Atoll in the Tuamotu Islands of French Polynesia on August 7, 1947. The successful conclusion of the raft's journey demonstrated that it was indeed plausible for South Americans to have reached Polynesia by traversing the immense expanse of the Pacific.

The Kon-Tiki expedition drew worldwide attention and was celebrated as a testament to human resourcefulness and resolve. It challenged the conventional understanding of ancient navigation and the origins of Polynesian civilization.

Heyerdahl's theory, supported by the accomplishment of the voyage, provided an alternative viewpoint on the settlement of the Pacific islands and the mobility of ancient societies.

Thor Heyerdahl's book "Kon-Tiki: Across the Pacific in a Raft" and a documentary film about the expedition further popularized his remarkable adventure. The Kon-Tiki narrative continues to symbolize adventurous exploration and pursuing hidden historical truths, as it represents the spirit of experience and the desire to expand the limits of human knowledge and comprehension.

Moreover, this expedition became one of the most celebrated expeditions of the 20th century.

Debunking Polynesia

One of the greatest questions in anthropology is how the shared customs, cultures, and languages among the inhabitants of Polynesia also ended up in Rapa Nui, Hawaii, and New Zealand. While a prevalent theory from the 1930s posited that the islands were progressively settled from Southeast Asia, only some were persuaded by this idea. This included the Norwegian explorer and ethnographer Thor Heyerdahl, who would later come up with the Kon-Tiki Expedition.

Heyerdahl proposed an alternative theory, positing that South Americans colonized Polynesian islands from the west using "drift voyaging" – constructing rafts with sails and relying on ocean currents. His key supporting evidence included the Moai statues on Rapa Nui (Easter Island), which he believed exhibited more South American than Asian cultural influence.

Additionally, the legend of Kon-Tiki Viracocha, a Peruvian chief who sailed into the Pacific on a balsa wood raft, bolstered his theory.

Although Heyerdahl's ideas were met with skepticism from most anthropologists, he decided to prove his point by embarking on a daring journey. He assembled a diverse six-man crew, primarily consisting of Norwegians and one Swede.

The team included Herman Watzinger, a thermodynamics engineer; Erik Hesselberg, a childhood friend and navigator; Knut Haugland, a telegraph operator with a history of wartime heroism; Torstein Raaby, another wartime telegrapher; and Bengt Danielsson, a Swedish Sociologist who served as steward and translator.

Together, they set out to test Heyerdahl's theory by replicating the legendary Kon-Tiki voyage.

Accompanied by his small team, Heyerdahl and his men traversed the Atlantic Ocean. They started from Morocco and ventured within 600 miles of Central America by using a replica of an ancient Egyptian reed boat called the Ra. This journey supported the idea that pre-Columbian civilizations in the Western Hemisphere might have shared an influence from Egyptian culture.

The team commenced their voyage on April 28, 1947, initially being towed by the Peruvian navy to avoid coastal traffic. They relied heavily on the Humboldt Current and trade winds and headed westward.

On July 30, 1947, the crew sighted land for the first time – the atoll of Puka-Puka. Five days later, after 97 days at sea, they reached the Angatau atoll. Here, they contacted the inhabitants but couldn't safely land the raft.

Their raft struck a reef days later, on August 7, 1947, and eventually washed ashore on an uninhabited islet near the coast of Raroia atoll. After a few days, flotsam from the raft washed up, alerting nearby villagers, who arrived on canoes to rescue the voyagers. They were later taken to the nearby island and warmly received with traditional feasts and dances. Shortly after, a French schooner towed their raft, transporting them back to Tahiti.

Controversies

Heyerdahl's interest in Polynesian and South American cultures inspired his "Diffusionism Theory." He posited that the original inhabitants of Polynesia might have come from South America rather than Asia, a view at odds with the beliefs of many scholars.

He also drew connections between shared cultural and botanical traits in both regions to substantiate his theory. His enthusiasm for the theory grew as he delved into ancient South American cultures. He argued that the conventional wisdom that Polynesians originated in Asia failed to adequately explain the commonalities between Polynesian and South American cultures.

He practically tested his theory via his raft, "Kon-Tiki," in homage to the Inca sun god Viracocha. He constructed it using materials that would have been accessible to pre-Columbian South American people. As the expedition drew extensive public attention, controversy and engendered enthusiasm within anthropology and exploration, contentious aspects of the journey followed.

Despite capturing the public's imagination, the expedition faced skepticism from scientists and anthropologists. Critics contended that the experiment did not prove definitively that pre-Columbian South Americans had settled in Polynesia. They argued that the crew's success could be attributed to their determination and the use of modern navigational equipment rather than serving as a reflection of the capabilities of ancient South American mariners.

The prevailing theory in anthropology, underpinned by genetic and linguistic evidence, supported the notion that Polynesians were descendants of Asian seafarers. This evidence indicated that Polynesian culture originated in Asia rather than South America. The Diffusionist Theory, while intriguing, stood in contrast to this scientific consensus.

Critics also pointed out significant cultural disparities between Polynesia and South America, including differences in language, art, and religion, which were not readily reconciled with Heyerdahl's theory. Questions then arose about whether the Kon-Tiki raft faithfully represented ancient South American rafts. While his raft survived the journey, doubts emerged regarding whether the materials and construction techniques were historically accurate.

Critics also contended that the successful voyage could be a more direct, non-stop journey from South America to Polynesia. Heyerdahl posited that ancient South American mariners could have engaged in "island hopping," a series of shorter voyages, to reach their destination.

This assertion raised inquiries about the practicality and feasibility of such a journey. Some even argued that the Kon-Tiki expedition's success might have been attributable to luck and survivorship bias. While Heyerdahl's team succeeded, previous mariners who may have attempted similar journeys could have perished, leaving no historical record.

It's worth emphasizing that Heyerdahl's theory needed more contemporary scientific validation despite the ongoing discussions and debates. The majority of scholars maintain their support for the established belief that Polynesians were derived from Asian seafarers.

While his theory remains unproven and is not widely accepted within the mainstream scientific community, some argue it retains validity for several reasons. For example, the theory was unique because it took an interdisciplinary approach, combining elements of anthropology, archaeology, and oceanography. His unconventional methodology encouraged scholars to explore alternative perspectives and challenged the established academic boundaries.

He also built on cultural and botanical parallels between South America and Polynesia. Although these similarities do not constitute conclusive evidence, they have continued to intrigue researchers and prompted further comparative cultural analysis studies. Though controversial, the Kon-Tiki expedition was a pioneering example of experimental archaeology. Heyerdahl's attempt to recreate an ancient voyage demonstrated the potential for early mariners to navigate the vast Pacific Ocean.

While the experiment may not have conclusively proven his theory, it opened new possibilities for understanding the capabilities of ancient seafarers. It further stimulated discussions that led to exploring alternative hypotheses and reevaluating established beliefs about Polynesian migration. This intellectual debate has resulted in a more comprehensive understanding of Pacific Island settlement patterns.

He also highlighted the possibility of ancient cultural exchange and interactions across the Pacific. This called for further research into the genetic, linguistic, and archaeological evidence that underlies the people of the Pacific.

While his theory's specifics have been challenged, it has encouraged researchers to investigate the broader concept of transoceanic connections in human history. Nevertheless, the continued fascination and discourse surrounding Heyerdahl's concepts underscore his work's lasting influence and valuable contributions to anthropology, archaeology, and exploration.

The Way Forward

Heyerdahl's voyage left a profound legacy in exploration, particularly in scientific research and popular culture. One of the impacts of the iconic expedition is challenging the beliefs about the Polynesian peoples' migration and their ancient maritime practices. While his theory isn't universally accepted, his journey served as an open invitation to expand research on their origins and culture.

Since Heyerdahl traveled on a raft made from balsa wood, he proved that exploration is possible and accessible. This concept called on scientists and archaeologists to examine and reexamine existing hypotheses.

It also reignited an interest in archaic seafaring methods, particularly explorations using only basic rafts. That interest would later turn into excitement that encouraged others to take on similar transoceanic voyages like the Kon-Tiki to develop new knowledge further.

New contemporary expeditions began challenging their inner Kon-Tiki, such as the Ra II Expedition in 1970. This voyage geared toward substantiating another of Heyerdahl's theories wherein ancient Egyptians might have traversed the Atlantic Ocean using reed boats from papyrus reeds. The Ra II embarked from Morocco and successfully reached the Caribbean despite encountering various challenges.

The Tangaroa Expedition years later, on the other hand, was a direct reference to Heyerdahl. In 2006, Torgeir Higraff attempted to retrace the Kon-Tiki Expedition path meticulously. He replicated the original journey as accurately as possible.

In 2015, the Kon-Tiki2 Expedition materialized in Peru. It reinterpreted the Kon-Tiki journey in the modern times. This time, the explorers used two balsa wood rafts instead of one. These rafts then sailed across the Pacific to Easter Island, focusing on shedding light on climate change-related environmental issues.

The Kon-Tiki Museum Expedition is the most recent in connection to Heyerdahl's. The Kon-Tiki Museum in Oslo organized the tribute expedition to commemorate and emulate the original trip on its 70th anniversary using a replica raft called "Tiki." This harnessed Heyerdahl's legacy to address modern challenges.

Heyerdahl, whose journey remains an inspiration for individuals and researchers to date, established him as a trailblazing explorer. His subsequent explorations and written works continued to shape the different yet related fields of geography, anthropology, and navigation.

Aside from its influence in the academe as a valuable case study, it is also celebrated and commonly found in popular culture, such as books, films, and travel documentaries touching on cultural and literary landscapes. Even Heyerdahl's memoir and documentary film became classics in their respective genres.

The contribution of Heyerdahl will always serve as a catalyst for the world regarding exploration and challenging conventional wisdom. Without the Kon-Tiki Expedition, the world won't be the same.

Were it not for the world's understanding of ancient seafaring, migration, and people, there would be no thirst for adventure or hunger for knowledge.

CONCLUSION

Survival is a more complex concept than people might think. There are so many layers to Survival that most people need to be made of. Survival is not just about living during the wreckage of whatever happened. It is also about living AFTER the wreckage of what happened. Just because you survived the event does not mean you survived it entirely. Survival does not end when you are saved; it ends once you have saved yourself mentally and emotionally.

That may take years, or it may never happen. Another layer of survival, besides one's mental health, is whether or not you can handle what comes after. Will you accept that the world continued even as you suffered?

Will you be able to stomach the consequences of whatever actions you did at sea? The thing about survival is that it is also about the aftermath because survival is continuous. We have to understand to be able to conquer it.

The main takeaway from reading these stories should be that anyone, and absolutely anyone, can survive whatever comes their way as long as they have the drive to do so. For Alexander Selkirk, his drive was God. He used his faith to propel him towards hope every single day. For the men on the Mignonette (except for Richard Parker, for obvious reasons), it was their families back home.

You must find your purpose, drive, or allow it to see you. This doesn't only fall under survival at sea but also in life. Life is just a vast ocean of emotions and experiences. So, once you find your drive and your purpose, then you will survive.

The last thing I'll leave to you from these stories is this: Survival is not only about the event but also the succeeding events that started from that trauma. Don't undermine your survival once you've gotten out. It happened. You conquered it, and now it is time to beat the next. Stick to your purpose, and things will fall into place with just some push.

WORKS CITED

- Britannica, T. Editors of Encyclopaedia (2023, August 28). cannibalism. Encyclopedia Britannica. https://www.britannica.com/topic/cannibalism-human-behaviour

- Posted by blogger in San Diego Ghosts. (2021, April 30). The Mignonette – A Case of Cannibalism. The Mignonette – A Case of Cannibalism - San Diego Ghosts. https://sdghosts.com/the-mignonette-a-case-of-cannibalism/

- HistoryExtra. (2023, June 21). Cannibalism at sea: the starving Victorian sailors who ate a cabin boy. https://www.historyextra.com/period/victorian/cannibalism-at-sea-sailors-ate-the-cabin-boy/

- N/A, N. (2022, February 21). The Macabre case of the Mignonette. Tales from the Quarterdeck. https://talesfromthequarterdeck.com/2021/11/26/the-macabre-case-of-the-mignonette/

- N/A, N. (n.d.). Quotes on Survival. Survival Quotes. http://www.notable-quotes.com/s/survival_quotes.html

- Magazine, S. (2007, November 1). Abandoned ship: The Mary Celeste. Smithsonian.com. https://www.smithsonianmag.com/history/abandoned-ship-the-mary-celeste-174488104/

- Tikkanen, A. (2023, September 8). Mary Celeste. Encyclopedia Britannica. https://www.britannica.com/topic/Mary-Celeste

- A&E Television Networks. (2023, August 23). What

- happened to the mary celeste?. History.com. https://www.history.com/news/what-happened-to-the-mary-celeste
- Sharda. (2022, December 29). The mystery of the mary celeste ghost ship. Marine Insight. https://www.marineinsight.com/maritime-history/the-mystery-of-the-mary-celeste-ghost-ship/
- Raunek. (2022, April 22). What are ghost ships? Marine Insight. https://www.marineinsight.com/life-at-sea/what-are-ghost-ships/
- Lucchesi, E. L. B. (2023, June 27). What are eerie ghost ships and how are they impacting the environment?. Discover Magazine. https://www.discovermagazine.com/environment/what-are-eerie-ghost-ships-and-how-are-they-impacting-the-environment
- Ratledge, J. (2022, July 27). The mystery of the mary celeste. US Premier ship Models. https://premiershipmodels.us/blog/the-mystery-of-the-mary-celeste/
- A non-profit foundation Dedicatedto preserving our Maritime Heritage. National Underwater and Marine Agency. (n.d.). https://numa.net/expeditions/mary-celeste/
- Seaver, C. (n.d.). A non-profit foundation Dedicatedto preserving our Maritime Heritage. National Underwater and Marine Agency. https://numa.net/about-numa-2/
- Whooley, D. (2014, November 12). 133 days at sea in an eight foot raft. meet Poon Lim. JOE.ie. https://www.joe.ie/fitness-health/133-days-at-sea-in-an-eight-foot-raft-meet-poon-lim-39850
- Blitz, M. (2017, October 26). The man on the raft: The story of poon lim. Today I Found Out. http://www.todayifoundout.com/index.php/2014/12/man-raft-story-poon-lim/

- Fitzgerald, C. (2022, June 22). Mess steward Poon Lim survived 133 days lost at sea. warhistoryonline. https://www.warhistoryonline.com/instant-articles/poon-lim-survived-133-days-lost-at-sea.html

- Yadav, S. (2018, November 24). Poon Lim, the Chinese sailor who survived 133 days stranded in the ... A Tale of Resilience: Poon Lim, the Chinese Sailor who Survived 133 Days Castaway in the Atlantic Ocean. https://www.ststworld.com/poon-lim/

- Young, M. (2020, September 21). Incredible tale of couple lost at sea for 117 Days. NZ Herald. https://www.nzherald.co.nz/world/maurice-bayley-who-survived-117-days-lost-at-sea-with-his-wife-dies-aged-85/B5OJDJYWD4773CQX24R5YBYZJY/

- Cerezo, A. (2019, November 1). 117 Days adrift: Full story. Castaway Channel RSS. https://paradise.docastaway.com/maurice-maralyn-bailey-117-days-adrift/

- from Wavelenght #82by Marine Trust. (2023, January 19). Survival at sea. issuu. https://issuu.com/marinetrust/docs/wavelength-issue-82/s/17930115

- Harriss, E., & Adrian. (2017, April 28). Maurice and Maralyn Bailey's 117 days at sea. Ripley's Believe It or Not! https://www.ripleys.com/weird-news/maurice-maralyn-baileys-117-days-sea/

- Benjamin, T. (2019, December 3). Brit who survived 117 days lost at sea on raft with his wife dies aged 85. The Mirror. https://www.mirror.co.uk/news/uk-news/brit-who-survived-117-days-21014862

- Cerezo, A. (2019, November 12). Getting to know maurice & Maralyn Bailey. Castaway Channel RSS. https://paradise.docastaway.com/maurice-maralyn-bailey/

- N/A, N. (n.d.). Quote by Martin Luther King Jr. Quote by Martin Luther King Jr.: "The choice is not between

- violence and nonviole..." https://www.goodreads.com/quotes/5042-the-choice-is-not-between-violence-and-nonviolence-but-between

- Military Order of the Purple Heart. (n.d.) Our Mission. Military Order Of The Purple Heart. https://www.purpleheart.org/

- Billy Graham Evangelistic Association of Canada (BGCEAC). (2017, September 17). Principal Photography Begins On 'Unbroken: Path to Redemption'. Principal Photography Begins On 'Unbroken: Path to Redemption' - The Billy Graham Evangelistic Association of Canada. https://www.billygraham.ca/stories/principal-photography-begins-on-unbroken-path-to-redemption/

- N/A, N. (n.d.). Quote by Herman Melville. Quote by Herman Melville: "There is, one knows not what sweet mystery about" https://www.goodreads.com/quotes/8010471-there-is-one-knows-not-what-sweet-mystery-about-this

- King, G. (2013, March 1). The True-Life Horror That Inspired 'Moby-Dick.' The True-Life Horror That Inspired 'Moby-Dick' | History | Smithsonian Magazine.

- https://www.smithsonianmag.com/history/the-true-life-horror-that-inspired-moby-dick-17576/?no-ist

- National Geographic. (2022, May 19). Nov 20, 1820 CE: Tragedy of the Whaleship Essex. Nov 20, 1820 CE: Tragedy of the Whaleship Essex. https://education.nationalgeographic.org/resource/tragedy-whaleship-essex/

- Sinrich, J. (2023, January 19). 35 Family Quotes That Hit Close to Home. 35 Family Quotes That Hit Close to Home | Reader's Digest https://www.rd.com/list/family-quotes/

- BBC. (2012, July 18). Shipwrecked by whales: The Robertson family survival story.

- Vosper, L. (2023, June 20). The Robertson Family Rescue.

The Robertson Family Rescue | NMMC. https://nmmc.co.uk/2022/05/the-50th-anniversary-of-the-robertson-family-rescue/

- N/A, N. (n.d.) Quote by Tom Althouse. Quote by Tom Althouse: "Fear not the unknown. It is a sea of possibilities" https://www.goodreads.com/quotes/3227082-fear-not-the-unknown-it-is-a-sea-of-possibilities

- The Editors of Encyclopaedia Britannica. (2023, October 2). Thor Heyerdahl. Thor Heyerdahl | Biography, Kon-Tiki, Ra, Books, & Facts | Britannica. https://www.britannica.com/biography/Thor-Heyerdahl

- The Editors of Encyclopaedia Britannica. (2023, October 2). Ra. Thor Heyerdahl | Biography, Kon-Tiki, Ra, Books, & Facts | Britannica. https://www.britannica.com/biography/Thor-Heyerdahl

- Fugelsnes, E. (May 18, 2022). Human skulls from Thor Heyerdahl expedition cause controversy. Human skulls from Thor Heyerdahl expedition cause controversy | Forskningsetikk. https://www.forskningsetikk.no/en/resources/the-research-ethics-magazine/2019-3/human-skulls-from-thor-heyerdahl-expedition-cause-controversy/

- Bruce, J. S., & Bruce, M. S. (1993). Alexander Selkirk: The Real Robinson Crusoe. The Explorer's Journal, Spring.

- Cartwright, M. (2023, August 25). Alexander Selkirk. World History Encyclopedia. https://www.worldhistory.org/Alexander_Selkirk/

- Howell, J. (1829). The Life and Adventures of Alexander Selkirk. Oliver & Boyd, Tweeddale-Court and Geo B. Whittaker, London.

- info@undiscoveredscotland.co.uk, U. S. (n.d.). Undiscovered Scotland. Alexander Selkirk: Biography on Undiscovered Scotland. https://

- www.undiscoveredscotland.co.uk/usbiography/s/alexanderselkirk.html

- Magazine, S. (2005, July 1). The real Robinson Crusoe. Smithsonian.com. https://www.smithsonianmag.com/history/the-real-robinson-crusoe-74877644/

- N/A, N. (n.d.). Top 15 lost at Sea Quotes: A-Z quotes. A. https://www.azquotes.com/quotes/topics/lost-at-sea.html

- Britannica, T. Editors of Encyclopaedia (2023, August 28). cannibalism. Encyclopedia Britannica. https://www.britannica.com/topic/cannibalism-human-behaviour

- Posted by blogger in San Diego Ghosts. (2021, April 30). The Mignonette – A Case of Cannibalism. The Mignonette – A Case of Cannibalism - San Diego Ghosts. https://sdghosts.com/the-mignonette-a-case-of-cannibalism/

- HistoryExtra. (2023, June 21). Cannibalism at sea: the starving Victorian sailors who ate a cabin boy. https://www.historyextra.com/period/victorian/cannibalism-at-sea-sailors-ate-the-cabin-boy/

- N/A, N. (2022, February 21). The Macabre case of the Mignonette. Tales from the Quarterdeck. https://talesfromthequarterdeck.com/2021/11/26/the-macabre-case-of-the-mignonette/

- N/A, N. (n.d.). Quotes on Survival. Survival Quotes. http://www.notable-quotes.com/s/survival_quotes.html

ABOUT US

Modern Daily Press focuses on crafted material especially for kids through subjects that captivate young minds - think action, adventure, and everything that sparks their curiosity!

Our commitment to producing high-quality content reflects our dedication to nurturing the love for reading and learning. Our team of passionate writers, editors, and illustrators work tirelessly to create books that not only entertain but also inspire.

From tales of epic battles to thrilling military adventures, we're on a mission to provide books that have the power to shape young minds.

Click the +Follow button on our Author Page join us as we embark on a journey of exploration and stay updated on our latest releases!

moderndaily PRESS

Exclusive Bonus Content

Dear Reader,

Thank you for your purchase. As an appreciation for your purchase, we added a **free audiobook download** for you. These files are available exclusively for free as .mp3 and can be downloaded by scanning the code below.

Listen for free on any smartphone, tablet, or PC device!

We thank you, valued reader, for choosing this book. We hope that it exceeds expectation as the author and team worked with utmost care to bring a quality project to life.

Should you encounter any issues, please don't hesitate to reach out — we are here to ensure you are fully satisfied with your purchase and look forward to meeting you inside the pages.

Love,

*Free bonus audiobook product may differ from images shown.

Review Club

FREE BESTSELLING BOOKS
☆☆☆☆☆☆☆

1 Leave a quick review of the book

USA CANADA UK AUSTRALIA

2 Download each week's FREE Kindle Book

DOWNLOAD

3 That's It. Thank you!

www.kindlepromos.com/club

moderndaily. PRESS   kindlepromos

Printed in Great Britain
by Amazon